The Abuse of Men

An Enquiry into the Adult Male Experience
of Heterosexual Abuse

Lynne Renoir

Lynne Renoir
PUBLISHING

© Lynne Renoir 2022

All rights reserved. No part of this book may be reproduced by any mechanical, photographic, or electronic process, or in the form of a phonographic recording; nor may it be stored in a retrieval system, transmitted, or otherwise be copied for public or private use—other than for "fair use" as brief quotations embodied in articles and reviews—without prior written of the publisher.

ISBN 978-0-6483043-3-3

Cover and interior design by Damian Keenan

Published by

CONTENTS

	Foreword by Sandie Sedgbeer	9
	Introduction	13
	Background to the study	13
	Reflections on the Study	17
	Literature Review and Data Collection	20
A	**Incidence and Forms of Abuse**	21
	1. Gender Comparison	21
	2. Forms of Physical Abuse	21
	3. Forms of Psychological Abuse	25
	4. Characteristics of Male Victims	38
B	**Reactions to Abuse**	40
C	**The Role of Society**	54
	1. The Police and the Lower Courts	54
	2. Family Law	55
	3. Social Attitudes	59
	4. Gender Roles	62
D	**The Construct of Masculinity**	64
	Discussion	68
	Conclusion	93
	Bibliography	95
	About the Author	99

Praise for
THE ABUSE OF MEN

"The abuse of men by women happens and hurts, yet it is rarely covered by the media or recognized as an issue in society. Author and researcher Lynne Renoir believes it is time to do something about it. Driven by her history as an abuse victim Renoir has published a thoroughly researched and illuminating study that explores this often-hidden phenomenon and reveals how these men are affected by it. Moreover, she calls out the social structures and cultural negligence that enable female-on-male abuse to occur. *The Abuse of Men: An Enquiry into the Adult Male experience of Heterosexual Abuse* is essential reading for counselors, therapists, wives, mothers, and those who love or care for a man."

— *GAIL TORR*

"Lynne Renoir's research on the abuse of men gave me a whole new understanding of the violence that men can also suffer, and told me more about how she was able to put her own experiences at the hands of men aside to try and help men who have had the same experiences as her."

— *GEMMA HANSEN*

"We hear the word 'abuse' and most typically assume a woman is the victim, yet domestic violence by women is rising at an alarming rate. Lynne Renoir's own experience of abuse made her an empathic and understanding listener and as she heard of more and more men suffering at the hands of their partners, she went on to research the abuse of men. This book may be small, but it is impactful and deserves to be read widely, by therapists and non-therapists alike."

— *E. HARRIS*

Foreword

Google the phrase "domestic abuse," and a shockingly high number of reports will confirm that domestic violence has increased dramatically over the past few decades, with sharp spikes occurring globally throughout the Covid lockdown periods. But even more shocking is that most stories and examples published feature women being abused by men. Of course, we cannot minimize the harsh reality of the level of abuse endured by millions of women across the globe. But neither should we fail to question why the idea of men being abused by women is rarely included in the discussion of domestic abuse.

In the late 1980s, I wrote a book called *Sex, Lies, and Love — How to Understand the Opposite Sex*. Part of my research involved face-to-face individual and group meetings with both genders, from whom I learned much. But it was the women that surprised me the most. Frankly, I was baffled by some of the (unsolicited) confessions I heard of their tactics to belittle, humiliate, or "get one over" their male partners. These included purloining money from their inebriated husbands' pockets and wallets after a night out drinking with male friends or colleagues.

Why would any woman do such a thing to someone she professed to love?

Some said it was a way of "getting back at their partner" for a perceived slight. Others got a kick out of confusing their man into thinking he had spent more than he should. A shamed husband, it seemed, was more controllable. As was a partner in the throes of desire — using sex as a bargaining chip was a common theme. Overall, I got the impression that many women, at least in that era, equated their intimate relationships with the opposite sex with wars they had to win. Still, none of the women I spoke with admitted physically abusing their men.

Now here we are, more than twenty years into a new millennium. And despite all the progress we appear to have made with equality, evidence of the abuse of men by their female partners is seldom covered in the media.

Why? How can this state of affairs have remained such a secret for so long?

Some of the answers can be found in the first-hand reports gathered and faithfully documented by Lynne Renoir in her Master's thesis, which provides the foundation for *The Abuse of Men*. Renoir's research confirms that men do not seek support as readily as women do. There are several reasons for this.

1. Men abused by their female partners often feel ashamed of their inability to maintain a masculine ideal that expects them to be tougher, bigger, stronger, more independent, and self-reliant than women.

2. Opening up about their situations often leads to ridicule. Renoir quotes a case in which a man who took his wife to court to regain access to his children was mocked and laughed at by a judge and jury members who refused to believe that women can be just as violent as men.

3. Since most research on domestic abuse historically focuses on abused women, little attention is paid to this inequity in training social workers, therapists, police forces, and social agencies. Hence, fewer resources exist to support abused men, and helping agencies do not know how to effectively reach out to and support them.

Yet, the statistics are alarming. According to a Special Report published by the US Department of Justice:

> "1 in 4 men have experienced physical violence by an intimate partner and 1 in 9 have experienced severe physical violence, sexual violence, and/or intimate partner stalking with impacts such as injury, fearfulness, post-traumatic stress disorder, use of victim services, contraction of sexually transmitted diseases, etc."
> *("Non-Fatal Domestic violence 2003-2012," https://bjs.ojp.gov/content/pub/pdf/ndv0312.pdf).*

In Britain, the national survey, "Domestic Violence: The Male Perspective," released in 2010 states:

> "About two in five of all victims of domestic violence are men, contradicting the widespread impressions that it is almost always women who are left battered and bruised."

Later surveys conducted in the UK have shown no significant reduction in these statistics. A more recent update provided by the British organization Parity, a national non-party charity that seeks changes in the law to redress statutory sex discrimination, warns:

> "The prescription of domestic violence as a woman's problem, and not a social problem affecting both sexes and their children, is now strongly entrenched in societal attitudes in most western democracies including the UK. It extends particularly to Government, local authorities, and other public bodies, including police forces, social agencies, children's charities, and even the judiciary. The result has been to largely ignore or subordinate the plight of male victims, and consequently support services for them are hugely inferior to those in place for female victims and geographically totally inadequate."

Abuse of any sentient being is a terrible thing. The abuse of women — and animals — is campaigned against in many societies. But the abuse of men by women remains largely a dirty secret. That such abuse happens more frequently than we know, and its effect on men and their children is overlooked, is both a tragedy and a travesty. Men are supposed to be able to take whatever a woman might throw at them. And yet, because of prevailing attitudes towards men, abused men are rendered powerless in society today.

The Abuse of Men may be a small book. But it highlights a vast societal inequality that urgently needs to be acknowledged, discussed, and rectified. *The Abuse of Men* contributes significantly to a dialogue that must become a much bigger international conversation.

> SANDRA SEDGBEER, Talk TV/Radio host, and author of *Sex, Lies & Love: How to Understand the Opposite Sex.*

Introduction

The abuse of men by their female partners is a serious social problem, largely unacknowledged by society. It has the effect of exacerbating a sense of disempowerment which many men experience today. This study explores the nature and extent of abuse against men, how they are affected by it, and the social structures which enable the abuse to occur. My hypotheses were that the pain men experience as victims of female abuse is of such a magnitude that they are often unable to bear it, and also that there is a widespread prejudice against men which works against a just resolution in situations of heterosexual conflict.

The origins of the bias against men lie in certain philosophies within feminism, which label a wide variety of historical and cultural developments with the single term 'patriarchy'. This simplistic reduction enables the proponents of these philosophies to condemn men as a whole for the problems of civilization.

Background to the study

My interest in this subject arose from my experience over the past twenty years in treating male patients with muscular problems. As I saw the pain in their faces and felt the tension in their bodies, some of these men began to tell me of the women in their lives who were treating them in ways which seemed to be negating of their sense of self and destructive of their ability to function.

In my research of the literature in this field I discovered that whereas studies of male victims investigate mainly physical abuse, those relating to the abuse of women cover physical, sexual and psychological abuse. I felt, therefore, that it would be appropriate to carry out a similar wide-ranging enquiry with regard to men.

My initial contact was with the editor of a men's magazine held in the State Library of New South Wales. He provided the names of various organizations which conduct groups for men. These fall into two categories: support groups, where men share their experiences in an environment of trust; groups which are open to the public (including women) and are working towards reform of the law and public policy. I forwarded to the convenors of these groups an information sheet about my research. This was circulated to members of the support groups either by post, email or at group meetings. I was invited to address meetings of the groups working for reform.

Included on the sheet was an invitation for men who had experienced abuse to be participants in the research project, and to phone me to arrange an interview. The limitations I imposed were that the period of the abuse had been at least twelve months and that the relationship had now ended. I did not want to include men whose sense of empowerment was such that they ended the relationship after the first abusive episode. Also I wanted to avoid creating additional emotional stress on men who were still living with the abuser.

Through unstructured interviews I asked the men to tell me their stories, with particular reference to their feelings about the incidents. I interviewed fortyeight men from the eastern mainland States, Tasmania and New Zealand. Twenty one interviews were conducted in Sydney in the homes of participants. For those who lived at a distance I recorded the interviews on the phone. The average duration of interview was one hour. For the protection of participants, all names and identifying particulars have been changed.

Reflections on the Study

In choosing the method of unstructured interview, I was seeking to enter as deeply as possible into the world of the participants. As I had been a victim of male abuse, I felt I would be able to empathise at a deep level with the pain and loss of self respect which an abused person experiences. I was strongly influenced by theorists such as Maslow, who advocates an I-thou relationship between the researcher and the subject involving a 'mystical fusion' in which knowledge of the other arises through becoming the other (Rowan in Reason and Rowan (eds.) 1981 p.84). Krieger feels that when we discuss others we are always talking about ourselves. She believes that we should 'see the world as self' (1991 p.5), and in this regard I found myself resonating with the participants' feelings of shame, anger and betrayal.

Since the participants had suffered abuse by a woman, my role as a female researcher was an ambivalent one. I found myself wanting to give to the men the kind of empathy which they had not received from their partners. I also wanted them to know that, as a result of my own experience, I understood the shattering effects of abuse. In the early interviews I disclosed what I had suffered at the hands of a man, but I then became concerned about a possible perception by participants that I might hold negative attitudes towards men, or even that I might be a radical feminist in disguise who would use the information against them. I then discontinued the disclosure on the grounds that it could influence the way participants presented material.

An assumption I brought to the research process was that the abused person must be given a voice. In my own experience, while I was 'under the roof' of the abuser, I had no rights. Had I disclosed to anyone what was happening I would have either been disbelieved or told to be submissive. Fine states that when we opt to engage in social struggles with those who have been oppressed, we probe how we are in relation to the contexts we study (in Denzin and Lincoln (eds.) 1994 p.72). It seemed to me that abused men are silenced the way I was, or if they do speak, they are not heard. A frequent question asked by participants was, 'You do believe me, don't you?', and they would offer to show me legal documents to substantiate their stories.

I refrained from asking participants whether their behaviour could have contributed to the abuse. That question might have had a place within a different methodology. In the context of this study, however, I felt that since abused men are constantly being blamed for their predicament, such an approach by a researcher would have been disempowering.

My unwillingness to investigate contributing factors in the behaviour of participants is an area of bias in the study, since it is possible that in some cases the stories were slanted against the abuser.

Although there were a few occasions when I felt there could have been significant contributing factors to the abuse, I was surprised by an attitude from several men who blamed themselves for behaviours which I felt were perfectly normal and acceptable.

This is consistent with the attitudes of those men in society who carry a deep collective guilt towards all women.

Researchers such as Olesen have raised ethical concerns about using participants as a means to an end (1994 p.166). The purpose of this study was not only to enter into the experiences of abused men, but to alert society to the pain they are enduring. To this end I am having the study published. At times the men seemed to experience a kind of enrichment from being able to tell their stories. Some of them could not get to the end without tears in their eyes. Krieger writes, 'People who let social scientists study them are giving an altruistic gift. They are contributing to the development of knowledge, not knowing where that development will lead or how it will impact on them' (1991 p.153).

Many of the participants in this study were well educated and had sought to work through their personal issues, either with a therapist or in support groups. Some of the findings will not be generalisable to those few men who seek immediate help and are able to find it, or to those who retaliate with violence.

Literature Review and Data Collection

My initial impressions about the way men are treated were supported by the literature, and led to a line of enquiry concerning male powerlessness. This is related to the way modern society functions, in terms of both its structures and its attitudes towards men, and in the conditioning to which men are subjected. The material from the interviews and the literature suggested an analysis under the headings of:

- Incidence and forms of abuse;
- Reactions to abuse;
- The role of society; and
- The construct of masculinity.

Incidence and Forms of Abuse

Gender Comparison

McNeely and Robinson-Simpson found that women have a higher mean and median rate for perpetrating severe violence than men (1988 p.186). A bibliography compiled by Martin Fiebert (1998) examines 95 scholarly investigations (aggregate sample size over 60,000) which show that women are as physically aggressive, or more aggressive, than men in their relationships with their partners.

Straus (1996) states that although women are more likely to receive injuries, men are more likely to be victimized by their wives. He claims that women also initiate violence rather than only becoming violent in response to their own victimization (cited in Mignon 1998 p.141).

Forms of Physical Abuse

Sniechowski and Sherven (1995) found that women more often use weapons than do men (82% of women; 25% of men). Cook states that according to a study of 328 married couples published in the Journal of Marriage and the Family, 'Women were significantly more likely to throw an object, slap, kick/bite/hit with fist and hit with an object' (1997 p.38).

In two Australian studies, the most common type of male behaviour which resulted in abuse was minor violation of household rules, and the three most common reasons women gave for abuse of their husbands were: to resolve the argument, to respond to family crisis, to 'stop him bothering me' (Sarantakos 1998; 1999).

The stories of the participants in this project confirm the kinds of abuse outlined above.

JASON: She would throw hard objects at me, like photos, bottles, plates. This would happen if I did things like not putting clothes in the proper place, or not hanging a towel up. If we were out and she wanted to go home and I didn't, she'd put on one of these tantrums.

KEVIN: She burnt a hole in my arm and hit me in the face with a cooking pot that split my eyebrow. She picked up a hunting knife and threatened me with it. I took that one off her and she took out another one and she threatened to cut my eye out and I could watch her kill Karen. We struggled for the knife and it went into her thigh. She then took out an AVO against me.

ANDREW: She'd throw things at me — whatever she could find — ash trays or anything heavy. Sometimes she seemed like a person possessed. She would grab me by the genitals. 'I'll rip your fucking balls off' she'd say. Then if I restrained her by holding her shoulders she would try to bite me or kick me.

BRUCE: Once when I was about to drive off to cricket, she put her head through the car window and smashed a dish of Farex in my face, cutting my eye.

ROY: I had to work long shifts and often when I came home, I'd find my wife had left the children (the youngest was only a few months) and had gone down to the club, drinking and playing the poker machines. Sometimes when I went to get her, she'd smash a glass or a bottle across my head. Several times I had my head cracked open.

STUART: She would get mad about anything at all and go off her head. She'd throw whatever was in her hand at the time — firewood, pitchforks, rocks. Once she threw a cup of hot coffee all over me. Then when I tried to run away she threw a glass bowl of nuts.

On another occasion she threw the cutlery container at me — knives and forks went everywhere. Then she picked up a carving knife and was trying to stab me. I grabbed her wrists and managed to escape. I ran to my car, but she ran after me with a glass in her hand and screamed, 'You get in that car and I'll break the windows'. Then she hit me with the glass on the side of my face. It severed my temporal artery. I was losing a huge amount of blood and she was still screaming at me.

IAN: She used to scratch me on the face and neck. One night I was lying in bed, half asleep. She came in, and with a full-blooded fist she punched me in the left eye. She had her engagement ring on and the huge stone nearly gouged my eye out.

EVAN: Her abuse? Hitting with fists about my face and body. Kicking my legs. Biting at my protective arms. Throwing shoe polish or bottles at my head. Poking me in my face and body while screaming in my face. Once she knocked me down from behind and bit my right hand badly.

GEOFF: After she'd blown up about some triviality, I would just keep quiet, but then I'd be subjected to three or four hours of ranting and raving on what I was doing wrong. If I tried to leave the room, it would result in something being thrown. It started with things like fruit, but then she'd throw things that belonged to me, or something that someone in my family had given me and it would get smashed — usually something made of glass. Then she began to throw things directly at me.

Once she threw the heater at me and it broke. But if ever I left the house, she'd lock me out. In the end I'd just sit there and agree to everything she said, knowing that within a few hours, if I was lucky, she'd run out of steam.

MICHAEL: Our baby was very sick, and I said she should take him to the doctor. She was furious that I should make a suggestion about the baby. She started screaming and throwing things all round the house. Then she said she would take the children and leave and she grabbed the car keys. I knew she was in no fit state to drive, but I was particularly worried about the baby, so I stood at the door of his room and would not let her get him. She went to the kitchen and came back with a carving knife. She stuck it into my stomach and I knew she was about to stab me. I held on to the blade and it cut my fingers to the bone. Then she went back to the kitchen and threw a pot with chip fat at me. It hit me in the forehead and I nearly passed out.

Abuse could sometimes involve misuse of property, creating danger, and damage to property.

ANDREW: One day I left the house, and when I came back I found she'd smashed my CDs.

RICHARD: Every time I went to pick the kids up for access, she would jump on to the bonnet of the car to force me to attack her to get her off.

GEOFF: I'd do everything I could to avoid arguments in the car. If she was driving she'd get worked up to a point where she'd suddenly veer to the other side of the road and drive straight at oncoming traffic or she would steer off the road at a telegraph pole. Or if I was driving she would suddenly pull on the hand brake or she would grab the steering wheel and the car would go all over the road. Or without warning she'd give me a backhander straight into the face.

ROBERT: She got some scissors and cut up my shirts. On one occasion she lay down on the ground in front of the car so I couldn't drive off. On another occasion when I tried to go to work she got on to the bonnet of the car holding the baby. One other time I was on a night shift and it was raining. She ripped out the windscreen wipers, which meant I couldn't drive. Sometimes she'd lock me in the house. She'd take my keys, my credit cards, my identification badge and my money — anything she could get her hands on just so she'd have something to negotiate with at a later date.

Forms of Psychological Abuse

In his work with abused men, Hoff has compiled a list of common behaviours of female partners. These include: embarrassing the man in front of other people; intimidating and threatening him; insisting that anything he wants for himself is selfish or wrong; frequently causing him to feel guilty and ashamed; preventing him from taking a job or doing a course of study; threatening to harm herself or the children if he leaves; blaming him for her behaviour; treating him as a servant; forcing him to leave social gatherings and restricting his contact with friends or family; causing him to feel constantly afraid and 'on guard' (1999 p.1).

Unreasonable and unprovoked verbal attack was the form of psychological abuse most commonly reported by participants.

MALCOLM: Sometimes she'd go down to the pub at 1.30 in the morning and stay there for hours. If I said anything about it, she'd put on a tantrum — like a young child, stamping her feet, going red in the face, shaking, and just losing it.

RICHARD: She stopped doing any housework. I went to work very early and she would sleep in and not bother to wake up and get the kids to school. They missed a lot of school. In the end I had to ring her from work to make sure she and the kids were up. But then she'd throw tantrums and take it out on the kids.

PAUL: A friend of ours had died. My wife said to me, 'I wish you had died instead of him'.

MERVYN: When she didn't get what she wanted she would resort to a tirade of verbal accusations and there were so many just in one sentence that I found it quite overwhelming. She would never give space to hear my side of the story or to any feedback about the effect of her behaviour.

RAYMOND: She had a gambling addiction and she would sit in front of the radio all day, seven days a week, listening to the races. When our son was born she completely neglected him. She couldn't be bothered feeding him or bathing him. I had to do everything. Then she'd scream and swear at me and tell me to leave him alone.

MARK: No matter how successful I was in my profession, she would make comments like, 'Who did the work for you?' 'Whose palm did you grease?'

ROY: Even worse than the physical abuse was the emotional. She used to say to me, 'They're not your kids anyway; you've only been a sucker; I've been having affairs with other men all the time'.

The woman's tone of voice and overall attitude was difficult for many participants.

MICHAEL: She just became cold and bitchy and cutting and all of the compassion just evaporated from her.

IAN: What hurt me most was her hostile attitude to me, particularly her tone of voice — it was always very stern and angry and vindictive. She was just so negative about everything I did or said. She'd exaggerate things to a ridiculous degree.

DEREK: She saw my own family and anyone I wanted to maintain contact with as competition. She would go into a whingeing, whining, carping, harping, nagging mood for days and weeks on end, in which she'd have bees in her bonnet about my mother, my father, my friends, my professional associates and this would go on and on.

Denigration was a feature of abuse. The man was made to feel inferior.

ALAN: What I originally saw as playful teasing turned into hostility and ridicule. She didn't like my body shape — I was too thin. She'd pick on anything: my colour sense was terrible; I had difficulty in describing exactly what I liked. Then the little niggles became enraged tantrums, the little slap became contemptuous bullying. My saying 'I don't like it' was taken as an insult from a cheeky child.

STEVE: She'd say, 'You're just a wog; my father warned me about wogs — you're all no good'.

TOM: I wasn't the right person. I didn't have enough money. I didn't have the right status. I wasn't smart enough.

WILLIAM: Nothing I did was right. I couldn't walk into the house without being criticised for something. She didn't like the way I walked, the way I talked, the fact that I was Australian. I did all the cooking and the housework, but she'd abuse me because I'd hung something the wrong way on the line, or I'd put the quilt on the bed the wrong way round.

LEN: Shortly after our marriage and from then on she kept saying, 'I don't love you. I don't know why I married you.' I was always trying to work out what I had done wrong. She didn't like my friends or my family so I distanced myself from them. I then felt I should do all the work around the house. I did all the housework, all the shopping and all the cooking, but it didn't make any difference.

GEOFF: Every time I was hanging the clothes out, she'd come and stand behind me and tell me I was doing it all wrong. If I hung clothes out when she was not there, when she came home everything I'd hung up the wrong way she'd pull off the line, put in the wash basket and say, 'You've got to hang those up again'. Then when the clothes had dried, she made me fold them a certain way at the clothes line — I was not allowed to bring them inside.

ADAM: Whenever I tried to fix anything around the house, she would say to me 'You stupid idiot, why can't you do this right? What are you, a dummy?' When it seemed that our first child would not be a brilliant student, she blamed me and said, 'he's stupid like you; your whole family are a pack of idiots'.

A common method used by abusive women is to place the man in a situation where whatever he does is wrong, even when he gives in to all his partner's demands.

NIGEL: She told me I had to work longer hours to support her, but when I did, she said I didn't spend enough time with her. I used to buy her things she said she liked, but then she'd abuse me for it. I rang to say I would be working back and I got a verbal bashing you wouldn't believe because I'd disturbed her; then when I worked back and didn't ring, she abused me for not ringing. I was in a no-win situation all the time.

GEOFF: Every Saturday morning she'd say, 'What are we doing today?' I'd say, 'I'm easy, what would you like?' She'd yell at me for not having an idea, but she wouldn't suggest anything. If I said, 'I'd like to stay home or go down the park and play with the kids,' that was the worst thing in the world. She'd rave on for two or three hours. What I was supposed to do was to guess what she wanted to do and then suggest it. When I managed to get it right, she'd respond, 'All right we'll do that, but only if you want to'.

Being humiliated in front of others was a painful experience for several participants.

JASON: She seemed to enjoy humiliating me in public, particularly when we were at the club. She would slap me across the face or throw food in my face. If we were having a dinner party she would make belittling, sarcastic remarks about me.

TED: I'm overweight and when we were out she'd refer to me as the hippopotamus.

GEOFF: One day I took the kids to the park while she went shopping. She came down to the park and started punching me in the face because we weren't home when she came back — a lot earlier than expected. There was blood everywhere — I thought she'd broken my nose. My kids were with their friends and they saw the whole thing. Some of the friends had their parents with them. So there she was with her audience and she played it to the hilt.

BRUCE: I used to play cricket on Saturday afternoon. Saturday morning was a nightmare because as soon as I started putting on my cricket gear she would start. One day she came to the ground itself and she kept screaming abuse at me on the field so all the spectators and players could hear it.

Sexual abuse included withholding sex as a form of punishment, or using it as a means of manipulation. Some women had a need to control and humiliate their partner by demanding sex at any time. If the man did not comply, they would go on the attack. Retaliation included emotional blackmail, locking the man out of the house, making disparaging comments that he had failed the test of manhood.

SCOTT: For her, sex was a system of rewards and punishments. It was not a way for us to communicate. If I did something she didn't approve of, she'd turn off sex for weeks. I was not allowed to just reach out and touch her. She would recoil and say, 'Why does everything have to be about sex?' She said to me once, 'If you really loved me, you would cut off your penis'.

ALAN: Because I had told her what aroused me, she would use that against me by forcing an erection. She'd demand that I have sex with her to prove virility, love, worthiness. 'What are you, a man or a mouse?' I wasn't sure so I did it like a machine. When I started to say 'no' it was an inconceivable impudence. So she ignored it and did her mattress mastery over and over. When it wouldn't get up any more by itself, she'd tickle it into action. Pushing her off would have meant even more derision, so I lay beneath her wondering about my sanity and wriggled to end my pain.

Prior to the interview, Alan had sent me what he had written about his sexual violation.

ALAN: The horror of being touched. The cowering on the edge of the bed with an erection I couldn't control. The terror of more bullying and being told to enjoy it or else more scorn. My stomach was sick like being hit in the groin. My balls hurt from being squashed. Nothing would stop her whenever she said I needed to prove my manhood. I couldn't run away — nowhere to go. I was so ashamed.

While in the middle of it, I had no means to make sense of the various contradictions that confronted me. Her sexual violation of my reluctant body had no name. Her demands were not simply an occasional inconsiderate insistence. This was a remorseless and frightening menace.

Women would often devise 'punishments' for their partners. These included disappearing from the house without explanation, sleeping in the spare room, treating the man 'like a boarder', not passing on messages, not communicating at all with the partner.

GRAHAM: If I forgot to put out the rubbish, I was sent to Coventry for two or three weeks. Then during that period I might commit some other minor offence which would mean another two or three weeks when she wouldn't speak to me.

WILLIAM: She would eat with the children but I was not allowed to join them for the meal. There would be no food prepared for me.

JASON: When she was screaming and swearing, I would leave the house. When I eventually came back, she would not speak to me for days.

BRUCE: Whenever she was unhappy about something she would disappear for a week or two and take our son. I never knew when I came home from work whether or not they would be there.

Inappropriate and improper misuse of money placed many men in a difficult situation.

RICHARD: She demanded my pay packet; then she would go on shopping sprees and spend all the money and there would be no food on the table. The bills were mounting up and we were getting further and further behind. When I said I would manage the finances and I asked her how much she needed to run the house and what she spent it on, she said, 'That's none of your business'.

PETER: She kept making demands that I earn more money, so I finished up working three jobs, seven days a week. But no matter how much I earned, she would spend it all on luxuries and abuse me because we were getting deeper into debt, but I was not allowed to put any restraint on her spending frenzies.

The powerlessness some men experienced was indicated by the fact that they were required to do all the work within the home.

TED: I was like a slave to her. I had to do all the work, but no matter what I did she wanted more and more. I felt she was manipulating me and taking away my defences.

GEOFF: Although I was working full time and she was at home all day, she'd make me do all the housework and the washing and ironing. When I came home from work there'd be nothing to eat. She'd say, 'I didn't know what you wanted for tea'. Then when I said, 'You know I'll eat anything', she'd go into a rage, and then I'd have to cook tea. This happened just about every night, so I finished up doing all the cooking as well — otherwise the kids and I would never be fed. Then after tea I'd have to bath the kids and put them to bed. At that stage she would disappear, and I never knew where she was.

Abused men are often completely under the total control of their partners, and have to be accountable for everything they do.

ROBERT: I told her I was going over to a friend's place to watch the football. She said, 'Well you've got to be home by midnight'. I explained that the Cup did not start till 1 a.m. She said, 'You're not allowed go to then'. So I didn't go. I always gave in to her. I had been living at her place for nine months but she would never let me have a key. She said I had to put my car in her name, which I did. I had been off work and she said I was not allowed to go back to work. She started threatening me with AVOs if I went back.

WILLIAM: The fact that I went to Tech two nights a week — she considered that as me going out, so in retaliation she felt entitled to stay out Friday and Saturday nights all night — she'd come home at 5 or 6 o'clock in the morning. I was not even allowed to discuss where she'd been or what she was doing. Yet I had to account to her every time I left the house.

A woman can maintain total power over a man by making threats involving his safety and wellbeing or that of the children.

MERVYN: As well as hitting me and scratching me, she used to threaten to burn the house down.

STUART: I began to realise that her going off her head was just a power thing. It was like — 'You do what I say or I'll go bloody bananas'.

ROBERT: She refused to let me go to work and for three hours she badgered me. She had a carving knife and placed the two children at the front door, which was the only one that wasn't deadlocked. Every time I moved towards the door she'd go for me with the knife. I was terrified the children would be injured. I sat on the couch and she came towards me again. By this time I had no will to fight it. I said, 'If you're going do it, just do it — just kill me — get it over and done with — I can't handle it any more'.

RAYMOND: She would kick me in the genital area, she'd bite me on the shoulders and scratch my face and neck. She'd threaten to kill herself if I didn't give her the gambling money. Then she'd threaten to kill our son. In the middle of her screaming fits she would tell me and my son that I wasn't his father, even though we both knew I was. She also threatened to have someone bash me up.

BRUCE: She rang me at work and said, 'If you don't come home now I'm leaving you'. So I went home and she obviously had no intention of leaving. Once when I was away I got a call at 2 o'clock in the morning and she said, 'Well I've drugged Thomas and drugged myself, so if you're not worried, well don't worry about it.' When I got home I found Thomas was OK.

Among the worst forms of abuse which a man experiences is a sense of powerlessness when his children are being abused or used as a weapon against him.

STUART: She used to smack my young daughter really hard with a wooden spoon. There were bruises all over her legs and buttocks. She used to cry and dance up and down with the pain. My daughter was using paint brushes and she kept putting them in her mouth. My partner said to her, 'If you like it so much you can drink it' and she forced the liquid down her throat.

RICHARD: She made the kids write down that I belted them with a big leather belt with a buckle on it — just so she could present it to the Court.

GEOFF: She made a scrap book of newspaper articles about men who have killed their children during access visits. She read this to my kids, or made them read it and showed them the pictures. The book also had articles about men who kill their ex-wives. My kids told me that when they said, 'Dad would never do that', she said, 'You won't be saying that when you're standing beside my coffin and your father's in jail facing murder charges'.

In the Sarantakos study (1998) there were a few cases when men tried to escape from abuse, taking their children with them, but the courts apprehended the 'kidnapper' and returned the children to their 'loving mother' (p.14).

Many men felt undermined, particularly in their relationships with their children.

FRANCIS: As our children grew older she gradually started to push me out of the picture. She would always correct me in my handling of the children and if I made a suggestion, she would say, 'Oh no, we're not going to do it that way'. I felt continually undermined — whatever I did was wrong.

BOB: She began treating me as nothing more than a boarder. She wouldn't speak to me at all. Everything I did or said to the children was ridiculed.

Several men believed that their partner's provocation was an attempt to cause them to retaliate physically.

JO: She would goad me for two or three hours at a time. I would go along with whatever she wanted to try to keep the situation placid. But she was relentless. Even when I left the house to go for a walk, she'd chase me along the street.

TED: She'd walk past me in the house and spit at me, obviously hoping that I would do something so she could call the police.

STEVE: She'd come up very close to me and she kept on saying, 'Go on, hit me, that's what you want to do, hit me, go on'. I was trying to get her to calm down. But she couldn't stand that — it would make her twice as bad if I spoke in a calm voice.

Some women seemed to have a need to keep their partners feeling insecure. If a man had counselling and began to define himself more clearly, the woman would feel threatened — sometimes seeing it as an attack on her, and would strike back. She would be even more insistent that her violence was entirely the fault of her partner. Methods of keeping a man in the relationship included a pretence of making the relationship work.

MICHAEL: On the occasions when she was willing to listen to what I had to say, she would become quite manipulative and say, 'You're 100% right; I'm really sorry, I'm a bitch', and she'd pretend to come all my way. She'd be exciting in bed and there'd be this outpouring of love and affection. But the next day she'd go completely against what we'd agreed.

MALCOLM: Whenever she felt like treating me like dirt, she would. But there were times when she would be really nice to me. That was what kept me in the relationship.

IAN: Each time she took out an AVO, when we got to the court house she'd say she missed me terribly and wanted me back, so the case would be dropped. And each time I'd be silly enough to go back to her. She had me on the end of a string.

HARRY: She was sinister and manipulative and calculating. When she felt she was about to lose me, she'd turn it on sexually just to keep me. Then the abuse would start again.

Sometimes a woman would try to persuade others that she was the victim.

ANTHONY: She then went to the kitchen and opened the window and she started screaming as though she was being attacked. The window was only a couple of metres from our neighbours' window. I went out into the yard and she still kept up the screaming. The neighbours saw me outside and realised what she was up to.

GEOFF: She started punching me violently. As I moved away one of the punches landed in the door frame and she broke her hand. She told everyone I had attacked her with a cricket bat.

The issue which many men felt most deeply was a sense of betrayal. They had opened themselves to their partner, shared their sense of inadequacy, their fears and vulnerabilities. The woman then used this information as ammunition against them.

ALAN: Her behaviour triggered off all those feelings I had that I was inadequate. She was very clever. She knew what my weak points were — that I was unsure of my competence as a social being.

TOM: Fundamentally I had an openness to my partner; there were no protections in place. In trying to cement the relationship I trusted her completely. But she betrayed that trust.

Characteristics of Male Victims

O'Donnel feels that female abusers tend to look for male victims who are either very logical or very idealistic. The abusive woman needs something immovable in the man's mind which she can destroy.

An English research study on thirty eight battered men states: 'The majority of men who are abused are not seven-stone weaklings with Amazonian partners. They tend to be well built, but not aggressive. They're the sort of men who don't want to hit a man, let alone a woman. So when the violence starts they know they are just going to have to stand there and take it, and that tension produces its own kind of terror' (Wolff 1992 cited in Peloche 1999 p.6).

Detective Inspector Sylvia Aston describes the victims of female violence as the most decent kind of men, the kind who would not hit back. But they feel weak because they think that they should hit back (Thomas 1993 p.213).

Elizabeth McMahon, a counsellor of sexual abuse victims in Melbourne, states, 'In the case of women who sexually abuse, the victim is in years of sexual bondage before telling anyone… The male being sexually abused by a female is usually a very vulnerable personality who feels absolute shame and worthlessness' (Thomas 1993 p.138).

Many of the participants in the study fitted the above descriptions. They were quietly spoken, non-aggressive men. When they were being attacked they exercised restraint, either removing themselves from the vicinity or reasoning with their partner in an attempt to calm her down.

The situation of powerlessness in which the men found themselves both enabled the abuse to occur and was an integral part of the way in which they responded.

Reactions to Abuse

The physical symptoms men have reported after abuse include stomach pains, high temperature, racing pulse, thought distortion, anxiety, panic attacks (Hoff and Easterbrooks 1998 p.1).

NORMAN: The effect it had on me was that my body became very tired and sore.

EVAN: I was constantly tight in the stomach. All my basic physical functions were affected.

MERVYN: I had a feeling in the pit of my stomach — a dread of having to go through the emotional trauma of interacting with a person like that.

MARK: By the time the marriage ended, I had become anorexic. I weighed less than five stone. I felt so bad about myself I would run a hundred kilometres a week, rain, hail or shine.

Perpetual fear and being 'on guard' were experienced by most participants.

MATTHEW: Each night when she came from work I would be tense and nervous. I didn't know in what way she was going to abuse me.

STUART: I was on tenterhooks all the time. I was always checking on what my young daughter was doing to make sure that my partner would not attack her. I got into this habit of not only doing everything she said, but never making a decision for myself. I was terrified I would do something wrong and she'd blow up. I could never be myself. I always had to be one step ahead, thinking about how she might react. I was always looking for dangers, looking for signs. I had to guess her moods.

BRUCE: When I came home from work and she was there, I would be just shaking, just waiting for her to go off.

In order to survive abuse, a man may block the memory of the experience because the pain of recall is too terrifying. If he were to relive the abuse he could become hysterical and be treated as a psychiatric case — the way women originally were (O'Donnel 1994).

Commonly expressed reactions by participants were feelings of lack of control and inadequacy.

ANDREW: The more outrageous her behaviour, the more I felt I could not handle the situation... A lot of men just close down emotionally. They can't even allow themselves to admit that they need love and tenderness and they're not getting it. If you ask for it in a relationship you're going out on a limb, because you're giving the woman power to say 'no'.

ALAN: Whatever I did or tried to become or whatever I said or however I behaved, I wasn't able to change the circumstances with anything that I could possibly do. I couldn't talk to anyone.

Nobody would believe the fact that I felt so awful about what was going on. I just felt as if I was inadequate — that I didn't know what to do, that

I couldn't do anything. I would try to do things just so I could hear her say 'Thank you'. But nothing I tried ever had the desired effect and so I felt even more inadequate.

KEVIN: I felt like an idiot. I didn't know what I was doing wrong or what I could do to make it right. She would never tell me anything more than, for example, 'If you don't come now I'll hurt Karen', and I would come home and she wouldn't even be here. I was losing time at work. It was making me feel stupid because I didn't know how to react to her and it was making me feel as if there was something wrong with me. I thought everyone else was managing their relationships, so why couldn't I get it right? So I started getting depressed.

NIGEL: She reduced me to a state of total powerlessness. I couldn't function as a husband, as a father. I did everything she wanted and got abused for it. The more I gave in to her the more she destroyed me. I became like a little man just towing the line. I had to ask permission to go and see a friend. I was just her slave in the relationship.

EVAN: I was disappointed that I could not be proactive about changing the situation. I felt stymied. There was a part of me that felt I should have been able to fix it. In the past it's always worked for me when I've used a reasoned approach. Why couldn't I get her to talk through the issues?

Constant denigration of the man could cause him to accept his partner's view of him and to lose self esteem.

MALCOLM: She made me feel totally insignificant. Whatever I wanted meant nothing to her. What she wanted was the only thing that mattered.

TOM: I had made her a part of my life at the very core. She had my complete trust. If she said something to me, I would believe her. So her view of me became my view of me. This sort of thing eats away at your self worth and isolates you from everyone around you. I had to give her everything she asked for because she set it up that I could be happy only if she was happy.

NIGEL: Self esteem? You don't have any self esteem. You take on board all the stuff she dishes out.

ANDREW: I felt less than a man because I couldn't find a way to handle her destructive behaviour.

ALAN: It was as though I was looking in a mirror but couldn't see anything. Whatever identity I had all of a sudden had vanished. I was working on automatic pilot. I didn't know any longer what it was to be a man.

SCOTT: My sense of self worth was affected because I was facing a problem that could not be solved. I also doubted my ability to 'do the emotional stuff' because I felt that women knew more about it than men.

WILLIAM: All the horrible things she said about me just gnawed away at me and at some level I must have believed them, because in the end I became what she told me I was. I wasn't interested in life. I became what she wanted so that she had an excuse to treat me that way. She never kept a single promise that she made to me. We would have a discussion and agree on a solution, but when the time came she would always find an excuse to break it — and it would always be twisted around that it was entirely my fault. I had to change. There was nothing at all wrong with her. I was made to feel worthless.

KEVIN: I haven't been able to work since we split up — three years ago. I don't feel like a worthwhile human being any more — no matter what my friends and family tell me. I feel like I am just such a worthless person, I don't even want to seek anyone's approval. A lot of the way I feel is tied up with the treatment I received in court and by the police. I was brought up to respect authority so when the authorities turned against me, I felt there was nothing left. The magistrate said, 'It's not the first time he's done it; it's just the first time we've caught him'. I walked into that court knowing I was a good person. I treated my wife with the utmost respect. But after that magistrate said that, I felt I was just an animal.

IAN: My self esteem has taken such a battering that I feel I could never trust myself to get it right in a relationship with a woman.

FRANCIS: I felt powerlesss — whatever I did was wrong. I blamed myself for not being able to get the kind of job she thought I should get so she could live in a really nice house. I felt she was not accepting my identity — I was not a smart businessman. I felt diminished by her attitude. I felt inadequate. I started to question my own judgment on things and my own worth as a person and my ability to achieve anything worthwhile. Part of me knew I could do better, but it was like — no matter what I did I couldn't get there. I felt like I was a failure in every part of my life — at work, in my marriage, as a father. Whatever study I did, she would see it as a waste of time. She showed no interest in anything in my life. I felt devalued.

DEREK: I found her behaviour humiliating and embarrassing. I took it on board and I was very hurt by it and it didn't do anything for my self confidence. All that tension she used to set up and the moods she used to get in used to depress me and I used to have to go to work in a very difficult and stressful job and try to perform in a public arena in a state of depression. I believe to this day that I did not become as confident in my profession as I expected myself to be because of what I went through during this period of twelve years of marriage.

ADAM: It got to the point where what self esteem I had, had gone. It just seemed like I believed within myself that I could not do anything. It got to the point where I was afraid to even attempt to do anything, because I knew within myself that I was going to fail — or she would tell me I'd failed. So it just wasn't worth trying. I was always doing my best, but my best was never good enough.

EVAN: I became sad and morose. I had always been an outgoing, gregarious person, but I found it difficult to make conversation with people. It destroyed my belief that I was a worthwhile person.

Counsellors report that abused men say to themselves, 'I am no longer a man', and spend most of their efforts hiding their 'soul shattering shame'. They lose confidence in their ability to carry out normal tasks (O'Donnell 1994).

MERVYN: In my relationship with Deborah, I didn't like to admit that I was scared — in fact it took me a long time to admit that I felt scared and was affected by her abuse. That admission was challenging to my own identity as a male. I could not even admit to my close and supportive friends how much her behaviour was hurting me. I felt ashamed about that — the fact that I had let it hurt me, and ashamed that I was vulnerable to her, that my life was a mess having got myself into that situation.

ANTHONY: When I asked my wife, 'Why are you trying to destroy me?' she said, 'I've kept your bed warm for fourteen years. Now it's payback time.' It sounded as though her whole relationship with me was nothing more than prostitution. I was destroyed.

BOB: I had a breakdown. I took three months off work, but when I went back I just couldn't do my job any more.

ROY: I became emotionally withdrawn. I couldn't think straight. I started making mistakes at work and one of these caused me a serious injury.

Many of the participants in the study came to believe that the abuse was all their fault.

TOM: When she started treating me like a sort of attachment, I thought I must have done something, but I didn't know what it was. She said everything that had happened — I was responsible for it. I never had the courage to tell anyone what she was doing to me.

ANDREW: I thought it must have been my fault because I had provoked her. I must have been a pretty bad person to trigger this in her. She had me believing that I was the total cause of everything.

STEVE: I thought, 'What's wrong with me; I'm working two jobs, coming home, bathing the kids, doing the housework — and still getting abused day and night; what am I doing wrong?'

SCOTT: Whenever she was unhappy, we would have to have a discussion about what I had done to cause it. I was made to feel responsible for all her feeling states.

PETER: I thought, 'Maybe I'm causing this — maybe I am a bad person'.

MICHAEL: She could always get me to feel sorry for her. She could manipulate me into feeling guilty.

MERVYN: I started feeling just terrible about myself. I was always trying to decide whether I had caused the problems.

MALCOLM: I started to feel in the end that maybe I was not such a good partner. I felt that I was no good for any relationship with a woman. She made me feel as though I was the biggest arse hole that ever walked the earth.

IAN: Although the logical part of your brain tells you that she's the one with the problem, at an emotional level you feel terrible. You ask yourself, 'Why is this happening to me? I must have done something wrong.'

Confusion and uncertainty formed part of the reactions to abuse. This was often related to the men's view of themselves and their role.

GEORGE: When you're trying to maintain a relationship you often don't see these terrible things happening to you the way a person outside would see them. I felt split. I think I felt I was doing everything I could, but still wondering what else I could have done.

JO: Why would someone I love so much want to hurt me emotionally, to confuse me?

STEVE: She would twist things that I said, she'd deny things that she had said, and it got to the stage where I thought I was totally mad. And that was what she was trying to do. I started to believe that I would not be able to do my job, which always involved danger.

TOM: I did everything I thought I was supposed to do as a husband. I couldn't understand… after all I still believed I had a wife. In the end I realised that 'us' never existed. You put into question whether you actually were that person because it's completely gone. Not only is it gone but what you believed in was actually a lie.

Part of the sense of powerlessness involved the absence of alternatives. It also led to intense emotional pain and feelings about death.

ALAN: I thought of my options. Lock her out of the house as she did to me? The cops would come and take me away. Complain of domestic violence? She was too pretty and dainty for that to work. Leave? I could not abandon my kids. I would rather have died, and thought of it. Fight back? Somehow I couldn't see myself doing it. I don't know if it was cowardice, chivalry or intellect saying, 'Lay a finger on her even once and all hell will break loose'. Murder her but make it look accidental? Its appeal did grow, unbelievably.

GEORGE: I was distraught. I was pretty close to suicidal.

ADAM: I found it hard to maintain my job, just trying to concentrate. I couldn't sleep at night. I felt cut out of life, lost, rejected.

TOM: I felt I was dying inside. The feeling is like a cancer that eats away at you every day until all you have left is pain that never goes away.

STEVE: Many times I thought of killing myself. She not only destroyed me when we were together, but stopping me from seeing the kids — my life was not worth living then.

JASON: I went up to South Head and stood on the edge. I was very close to letting myself fall.

ROY: It got to the stage where I couldn't take it any more and I decided to commit suicide. I jumped off the bridge, but somebody saw me and got the police and they dragged me out.

In a study of abused husbands, Gregorash states that they believed they had tried everything to deal with the situation, but their inability to cope with it left their wife with total power over them. They were in a hostage-captor type relationship (1993 p.92). Some men would promise to do whatever the partner demanded, accept responsibility for untrue accusations, or make excuses for the partner's behaviour (Eldridge 1998 p.2).

ROBERT: Even after all this, I couldn't help feeling it must have been my fault, just as she said it was. She could manipulate anything I said to make it look as though I was to blame. I was no match for her. In the end I would just give in and say 'yes' to whatever she said, and of course that just made her worse. She'd say, 'See I told you I was right all along; you're lying to me'. I couldn't win if I agreed or if I argued. In the end it was easier just to agree.

MICHAEL: I was always aware that my acceptance of what she would and wouldn't tolerate was the predominant factor of peace. If I bucked the system there was less peace. She didn't change; I had to. I was always aware that no matter what I did, no matter where I put the resistance, nothing ever changed.

In the study carried out by Sarantakos (1998), family members were interviewed to ascertain the validity of the husband's account. 'The statements of the wife's parents and children confirm the husband's assertion that he lived in fear, that he was constantly intimidated and that he experienced demoralisation and powerlessness in his everyday life' (p.16). Some children reported hiding their battered father under the bed to prevent further injuries, or they would hide him in the store room or in the neighbour's garage.

Men are placed in a difficult situation in defending themselves. Part of being seen as a 'real man' in our culture is the ability to be able to take it, particularly from a woman. Since most men are taught never to hit a woman, even in self-defence, when they are attacked, they are rendered powerless (Sniechowski and Sherven 1995).

PAUL: When she slapped me across the face, I didn't really see that as abuse because everyone seemed to think that a woman could hit a man but never the reverse.

O'Donnel (1994) says that when abused men strike back physically, they describe this as the worst abuse of all — the destruction of the limits they have imposed upon themselves. The methods men use to attempt to diffuse or avoid potentially violent situations include: locking themselves in a safe place; getting home late; staying at a friend's place but without divulging the reason; sleeping in the car, shed, garage or wherever they can find shelter.

PETER: Every time she got out of control and became violent and hysterical, I'd leave the house and I'd sleep in my car or at the beach. This would happen a couple of times a week.

KEVIN: I took all the overtime I could get so I could get home as late as possible so she wouldn't abuse me.

As a result of prolonged abuse, men can lose belief in standards of morality.

KEVIN: If I can spend 25 years doing good and still get punished, what's the point of trying to do anything good for the rest of my life.

BOB: I used to try and teach kids that they should always do the right thing, but after what happened to me, I just didn't believe in anything.

Many of the participants found it hard to maintain friendships.

WILLIAM: She expected my whole life to revolve around her — what I wanted was irrelevant. I lost all my friends. I was not allowed to join them in any activities — or if I did, she would not speak to me for days on end — she'd just pretend I wasn't in the house.

SCOTT: Almost everything I did that wasn't done with her constituted a threat to her. By the end of the relationship I had no friends. I had no outside activities. I had nothing, because everything that I was interested in, every friendship I had, threatened her. She would make things so difficult for my friends that they just drifted away.

The man's feeling of powerlessness was an underlying reason for his failure to report the matter or to leave the relationship. Vogel suggests that a man may come to believe what an abusive woman says to him: 'You're crazy and stupid; no one will believe you; the police will never arrest me' (1996 p.21). Women are ten times more likely to report domestic violence against themselves to the police than men are (LFAA 1998 p.3).

The situation for men in abusive relationships is compounded by their lack of options. They are usually reluctant to leave their children, who are often victims themselves. Overberg says that women who abuse men are likely to abuse their children as well (Cose 1995 p.208). Abusive women take advantage of the man's powerlessness and his feelings of protectiveness towards his children. Being brought up to see himself as the protector of women and the family can cause a man to believe that by leaving the relationship he is abdicating his responsibility. So men decide to stay and take 'whatever the women dish out to them' (Cook 1997 p.60). A further problem is that there are no shelters for the abused man (LFAA 1998 p.9).

When abused men seek help they are laughed at or scorned and they become extremely embarrassed. They are seen as weaklings or cowards. Because they know this is the way they are portrayed by society, they are reluctant to disclose their predicament through fear of further ridicule and being blamed for their situation (Easton 1998). Men deny that they are being abused in the belief that they are supposed to be able to handle it. They claim it is not a 'real problem' and they will offer other explanations for evident injuries. Daly and Wilson state that the most unreported crime is not wife abuse but husband abuse (1988 pp. 519-524).

The powerlessness which abused men experience within their

relationships could not occur unless such abusive behaviour was tacitly accepted within the community.

My enquiry led me to examine the ways in which our social structures discriminate against men.

The Role of Society

The Police and the Lower Courts

Several participants said that when they tried to report their abuse to the police, they were disbelieved, scorned, or had every obstacle placed in their way. Typical police responses were: 'What sort of a wimp are you to let a woman hit you?'; 'Run away and stop wasting our time'; 'You must have done something terrible to her to deserve this'; 'Look at the size of you! Maybe she was just defending herself'.

Whereas a woman can obtain an Apprehended Violence Order almost immediately and without any requirement of proof, the police view in many cases is that a man should be able to cope with the kind of abuse a woman might engage in. In most cases the police are required to arrest someone if they believe domestic abuse has been committed. There is often little effort made to find out who was the aggressor. 'Even if the man has a split lip and the wife is drunk and out of control, the man is likely to be placed in jail' (Cose 1995 p.209).

STEVE: The Chamber Magistrate said to me, 'You're supposed to be the stronger one — to be able to take strong hits. If you go ahead with this, they'll laugh you out of court'. Even if you've got a bloody nose and bruises, if you're a man, they say you have to have more proof to get an AVO.

MICHAEL: The next thing I knew there were two police officers at the door. They saw the lump on my head, the black eye, and the bleeding and I told them what had happened. They said my wife had made a complaint that I had assaulted her, so they handcuffed me and put me in a paddywagon. At the station the police said there was 'a high degree of probability' that I would assault my wife again!

KEVIN: I made two attempts to report her assaults to the police and they didn't want to know. One officer said to me, 'For your sake and for ours we might as well not drag this into court. The magistrate won't believe that a woman is capable of something like that'.

JIM: She would violently attack my 5 year-old son. Once she had him pinned to the floor, with her body weight on top of him. I would often try to separate him from her, but eventually I became afraid for his safety and I reported the matter. She then took out a restraining order against me, claiming I had threatened her with a gun. From that time onwards, neither the police nor the courts would listen to anything I tried to tell them about the danger my son was in.

Family Law

Regardless of the degree of abuse sustained by a husband, courts will nearly always award custody of children to the wife (Cook 1997 p.62). Only one in six men who apply for custody of their children eventually gains it. The Family Court in Australia normally elevates the mother to the role of primary parent. The father is seen as the 'disposable' parent (Green 1998 p.xi).

The Court is also reluctant to grant joint custody. Commenting on the bias against men in custody decisions, a retiring Family Court judge stated, 'The woman has had all the power; the man almost none' (Arndt SMH 19/8/00). Men are usually given only limited access to their children. Often they lose contact with them altogether because of the court's unwillingness to impose severe penalties on women who deny access (Arndt 1995 p.226).

A study by McMurray and Blackmore found that 81% of men described their former partners as obstructive, undermining and uncooperative when it came to arranging access visits (1993 p.154). Several researchers have linked the loss of relationship between fathers and children to the male suicide rate (Ambrose et al. 1983 cited in Smith 1998 p.24). The loss is also reflected in a recently-established psychological condition which manifests as reactive depression, termed the 'involuntary child absence syndrome' (Jacob 1986 cited in Smith 1998 p.12).

Cose quotes the words of a counsellor:

'I've found it easier to console people with cancer and AIDS than to console fathers who have lost all contact with their children… It is one of the most devastating things that can happen to anybody… They can't get over it. Their children mean more to them than anything else in the world. (1995 p.15)'.

When a woman is violent in a relationship, the court will not necessarily assume that she is a bad mother. If a man is seeking custody of his children due to his wife's violence towards him and them, he is usually advised by his legal representative not to mention the violence, or the judge may conclude that the man is a 'wimp' and, therefore, an unfit parent (Cose 1995 p.217).

Should a man try to protect himself from abuse, his wife may claim to have been assaulted and take out an Apprehended Violence Order. One of the most serious threats men face today is false accusations of sexual molestation of their children (Cook 1997 p.62). Lawyers report that denial of access, Apprehended Violence Orders and false sexual allegations are common strategies in the armoury of custodial mothers who want to limit or terminate children's contact with their fathers (Green 1998 p.213).

Some of the worst forms of abuse against men involve the Family Court, vindictive women, and questionable legal practices. From several sources I heard that there were a number of practitioners, known to lawyers, who could always be relied upon to supply whatever evidence was needed to support a woman's claims of violence against her or of sexual molestation of her children. The Court rarely imposes penalties on a woman who makes false allegations, even when she does this repeatedly. Each time a sexual allegation against children is made, the man is usually denied access until such time as the Court resolves the matter.

BOB: After the separation, she continually frustrated my attempts to gain access, but the Court didn't do anything about it. Then she took the children interstate so I couldn't see them. She claimed I had sexually abused my daughters, that I'd hit her over the head and belted the daylights out of her and pulled her hair out. All our friends and neighbours knew the violence went the other way.

GEORGE: My wife would not let me see the kids. She claimed I was violent. Later the judge said there was no evidence I had ever assaulted her, but there was evidence that she had been violent to me. Then she accused me of sexually molesting my daughter. I was devastated. I didn't see my kids for ages until the Court finally decided I could see them. Then she again accused me of sexually interfering with my daughter. So again there was a long delay. After a Court hearing which lasted ten days, the judge found that my ex-wife herself had molested my daughter in an effort to generate evidence against me. Despite this, she was still allowed custody. And the Court and the child welfare agency refused to take any action against her.

JASON: The pain of not being able to see your child is far worse than any abuse a woman gives you in a relationship. It's even worse than the death of a child, knowing your child is alive and you can't see her. It's just unending suffering. When I see children in their school uniforms and I'm not allowed to see my child… the pain is indescribable.

CHRIS: She then abducted my daughter to Europe. I received little help from the authorities here. Their attitude was that nearly all women who take their children out of Australia are fleeing from a violent man. This lack of co-operation has been experienced by many men I know in this situation. They don't seem to understand anything. Justice Nicholson said on the 7.30 Report, 'Oh yes, the Court is aware there is a problem [of false allegations] but no woman would ever knowingly falsely accuse a man of sexually abusing a child. They just imagine it is happening.' On the question of women denying men access, the Law Reform Commission said there was no real problem!

GEOFF: What happened to me has happened to a lot of men I know. Where the man is applying for joint custody, the woman ceases all forms of communication with her partner a few months before the Family Court hearing, so she can say to the court, 'There is no communication between us'. The judge then declares that joint custody is impossible and awards custody to the mother.

After a separation, when the man tries to go back to the house to claim his personal property, the woman takes out an AVO and he is barred from the house. The man's property then 'disappears'.

Social Attitudes

Woodstra (1994) reports that a man who had been assaulted by his wife was being treated in hospital, where his wife admitted her guilt to the hospital authorities. Yet the police laid no charges until he pressed the matter. When he told his story in the Family Court in Toronto, the courtroom burst into laughter, including the judge. The man then dropped the charges.

McNeely and Robinson-Simpson state that men increasingly are defenceless, both socially and legally, when allegations of domestic violence are made (1987 cited in Mignon 1998 p.140).

Domestic violence is an issue framed in the media and in the political arena as one of male perpetrators and female victims (Gross1992).

According to O'Donnel (1994), the American psychological community denies the existence of abused men. Sarantakos (1999) states that in Australia a negativist attitude to husband abuse is sustained within the training schools of professions such as social workers, social welfare officers and counselling psychologists, most of whom have learned to interpret domestic violence as wife abuse. Sniechowski and Sherven (1995) feel that our culture as a whole has a deep commitment to the belief that women are helpless and innocent.

Abuse of men is treated in the way that rape used to be, with victims considered to be as guilty as their attackers. Men are disbelieved, ignored or treated with hostility (Thomas 1993 p.203).

When men who have been abused report the matter to telephone counselling services, they are told to seek psychiatric help — not for the abuser but for themselves.

In his work with battered husbands, Thomas states that in all cases where the relationship ended in divorce, the wife had convinced the police, social services, legal advisers and courts that she had been the victim (1993 p.195). Society excuses female violence against men on the grounds that they are supposedly more aggressive because of testosterone, and are stronger and larger (O'Donnel 1994).

KEVIN: I've put myself in my own prison because I don't want to have any interaction with society any more. I feel too vile, too dirty, because the mainstream of society says this kind of behaviour from a woman is OK.

In all areas of life, men are viewed more harshly than women. This is reflected in the attitudes of professionals, law enforcement agencies, the media, and society as a whole.

DAVID: The culture denies that the man needs help after the breakup of a relationship, or indeed, on how to function in a relationship. Therapists are not trained to look at gender issues from a male perspective — not even male therapists. They are taught about female specific recovery or people recovery, not male recovery. The culture presents women's and men's abuse in a different way. It's hard to describe female abuse unless its classically male — bashing you up or something. Often it's more covert and the damage is a lot harder to trace. When I originally told a therapist I was sexually abused by a woman, he said, 'That can't happen — you're a man'. Another one said, 'Just forget about it; get on with your life'. That kind of response would never be given to a woman, but it is typical for men.

ALAN: Who to talk to for advice — family or friends? No way. I looked up the Yellow Pages. The voice answering the phone at the Rape Crisis Centre said, 'Only women are abused'. I spoke to a doctor. She seemed to listen to my stammering for a few minutes and then while scribbling asked, 'What are you doing to make her behave that way?'

ANDREW: Even after a lot of therapy I still feel that somehow I must have caused it all, because there is a big part of me that can't accept that women are bad. So if women are good and one of these good people does terrible things to me, it must be my fault; I must be bad. I think because society doesn't accept that women can be abusive, if a woman is like that, she can't accept that she's like that. Society says that women aren't aggressive — women don't attack men. So if a woman attacks a man, it couldn't possibly be aggression — it's justified behaviour.

MALCOLM: When you're trying to be a good person and good partner and a good father and you get trashed — to me that's abusive. But our society doesn't see it like that.

EVAN: I phoned the domestic violence help line to try to resolve some issues concerning the abuse, and the woman who answered the phone said, 'If you admit that you are the perpetrator and your wife says she has been victimised, then we can help you'.

DAVID: After I had ended my relationship with this woman, she still had a key to my house. She kept on letting herself in when I was home. I managed to persuade her to hand over the key. I had a spare one hidden. She found it and began to use that. I felt I was being stalked. I would wake up in the morning and she would be in the house. But as a man I don't have any right to use the power that I have — which is physical. If I had thrown her out the door she would have gone to the police and they would have said, 'What did he do to you?' and I would be in jail. I stopped leaving a spare key outside, and then one day she smashed the front door in. It was as though she was telling me that she owned me. I had no privacy, no sanctuary from her — not even my own bed. My programming as a man meant that I was unable, physically, to push her away. A woman can overpower a man and he has no recourse in society. Therefore, he has nowhere to go.

Gender Roles

From the literature and from the data, it seems that men believe women are valued more highly than they are, and that men are at a disadvantage in their heterosexual relationships.

ANDREW: Something that comes up a lot in men's groups is that men seem to need women more than women need men. Maybe the fact that women are so self-sufficient means we see them as superior to us. We need them so much we put them on a pedestal. And women will assume that role quite naturally. And then men feel diminished by that.

MERVYN: Men feel it's not manly to ask for help and support. If I don't play the traditional male role, if I admit I've been abused, I am vulnerable — my masculine identity is called into question.

DAVID: Men are conditioned not to read books about the emotions — we're supposed to do all the rational stuff. Men are disempowered emotionally; they are taught to not have emotional expression and outlets — and they're not supposed to have friends they can talk emotionally to.

One of the results of feminism is that it gives this idealistic view of women in that they are supposed to look at their victimship but they're not supposed to look at the way they use power. If the woman is always the victim, the only way she can solve the problem is by asserting herself. So if she's in the dominant position the man must have failed her in some way. But if she's in the submissive position then the man again is the one who's failing.

The idea of 'no means no' only applies when women say it. I find myself in a position where I feel tongue-tied in validating my own state. There is a hidden agenda that if a man wants sex, the woman is quite at liberty to say 'no', but that if a woman wants sex, the man should always say 'yes'. Also women can flaunt themselves sexually in any way they please and there is no responsibility attached to that. If a man were to do something similar it would be a crime.

The powerlessness men experience as a result of female abuse and social structures and attitudes is compounded by the conditioning society imposes upon them.

The Construct of Masculinity

Hudson and Jacot describe the phenomenon of the 'male wound' which arises from the fact that at a very early age boys make a psychological transition away from the female norm (cited in Thomas 1993 p.36). Whyte suggests that from the time they are weaned, boys, unlike girls, are not comforted but are taught to go off and handle things alone. This lack of acceptance of a boy's feelings interferes with his understanding of himself (1997b p.1).

When a boy relinquishes the bond with his mother to show the world that he is not feminine, he will be fearful of any traits, particularly emotionality, which are identified as feminine. He is left 'open, vulnerable and unprotected' (Goff 1998 p.5). In tribal culture the boy is initiated into the world of the adult male. Since our culture has no rite of passage into manhood, the young man rages against the mother in a defiant show of strength, to ward off the threat of being absorbed or smothered by the mother (O'Connor 1993 p.28). The process of rejecting the nurturing female world is seen by McLean as deeply scarring to the boy (1996 p.15).

Masculine behaviour seems to offer a security to men. It is like a mask which covers up what is really underneath, often an insecure man with a 'fragile sense of gender identity' (Formaini 1990 p.13). The lack of help to grow into a man and the resulting desperate clinging to an 'I'm fine' facade has disastrous consequences. Men's difficulties are with isolation. The enemies, the prisons from which men must escape, are loneliness, compulsive competition, and life-long emotional timidity. Men who display anger are covering up feelings of fear and loneliness (Biddulph 1995 p.24).

'If a boy is four or five, he's told he's not supposed to cry. He's not allowed to play with girls, because if he does, he's a cissy. He can't hug boys, because if he does, he's a poof. He can't hang around with Mum, because then he'd be a mother's boy, and he can't hang around with Dad, because he's not there. So from then until the age of eighteen he's officially dissociated from the human race' (Thomas 1993 p.263).

'Most men don't have a life. Instead, we have just learned to pretend. Much of what men do is an outer show, kept up for protection… A boy's spirit begins to shrivel very early in life, until (often as not) he loses touch with it completely. By the time he becomes a man, he is like a tiger raised in a zoo — confused and numb, with huge energies untapped. He feels that there must be more, but does not know what that more is. So he spends his life pretending to be happy' (op.cit. p.1). 'Manhood requires such a self-destructive identity… a shrinkage of the self, a turning away from whole areas of life, that the man who obeys the demands of masculinity has become only half-human' (Horrocks 1994 p.25).

Farmer describes men as the 'walking wounded' (1991 p.3). When the wounds remain unhealed men carry lasting pain, even though it is hidden behind a façade of male bravado. When men deny their emotions, they can easily believe that only women have 'feelings', or more accurately, that they don't (Goff 1998 p.1). The only emotion they are allowed to display in public is anger, and although men are intensely emotional, this realisation is hidden from them (McLean 1996 pp 20-21). McKissock believes that failing to feel one single emotion can lead to a shutdown in the full spectrum of feelings — including anger (cited in Biddulph 1995 p.185).

In discussing the question of their conditioning with participants, I found that it affects men in different ways. They can be totally cut off from their emotions, sometimes through fear of what could happen if they allowed themselves to feel anything, or they can experience intense feelings but believe that it's 'unmanly' to display them. Another response is that having been taught not to express emotions in childhood, they may have difficulty in giving a name to what they are feeling. In general, the men felt that their conditioning increased their sense of powerlessness.

ALAN: I did not have a language to describe the feelings I had. I believe that when a boy has to repress his emotions, he fails to learn a language to describe what he is feeling, so that in adult life he is like a stranger to his emotions. The normal conversations one has with oneself I couldn't have because I didn't have a language to describe it. If someone has asked me how I felt about the situation, I wouldn't have known how to answer them. I suppose bewildered. Because I had always needed to explain things to myself and found that I couldn't, I felt very frustrated with myself for not knowing what was going on. I'd be conscious of great anxiety, that there was something wrong, that I was not enjoying it — but I could not have described it to anyone. It's only in recent years that I've realised it was abuse.

ANDREW: Men don't give each other the emotional support that women give each other, so if the woman is the only source of that in a man's life, when she withholds it, he is terribly alone.

DAVID: For a heterosexual man to get affection and love (not sex), he can only get it from his partner when she says 'yes'; he can't get it from any other male or he'll be called a homosexual — even more by women than by men, and he can't get it from any other woman — and remember I'm only talking about affection. But the male then gets so needy for human physical contact of any sort that he comes to believe that sex is the only way that he can get it. The woman then has total power over him in that area. A woman can get affection from a range of females, but a man can't do the same. A man can become desperate for sex because it's the only way he can get his needs for affection met. Then the man is told he is bad because he's obsessed by sex.

Discussion

The sense of powerlessness which men experience, both in society and as a result of abuse by their female partners, will be discussed in terms of disempowerment, judgment and identity violation. I will critique feminist philosophy in terms of its effects on men, and analyse archetypal patterns in gender relations today.

The theoretical perspective in social science which addresses issues of powerlessness is Critical Theory. Its ontological basis is modified realism, where objectivity is located in the historically and socially formed patterns arising from human struggle. It concerns the interests and values in a particular society which help shape its dynamics. The epistemological position of Critical Theory is subjectivist. Knowledge is historically situated and truth is whatever leads to empowering for individuals (Le Compte in Guba (ed.) 1990 p.252).

Critical Theory seeks to uncover the causes of distorted communication and understanding and to render individual and social processes transparent to the actors involved, thus enabling them to pursue their further development (Smith in Guba (ed.) 1990 p.181). Habermas uses the traditional Marxist category of alienation, i.e. all forms of human activity which are determined by external forces rather than by the agents themselves (Dews 1999 p.5). He believes there is an emancipatory interest of a pre-theoretical kind which is anchored in social reality itself. The process of self-reflection is seen as an expression of that interest.

In drawing on the ideas of Critical Theory, I was seeking to explore the alienation which men experience today. This results from a perspective which has come to form part of our culture that men are the oppressors; they are responsible for all the ills of society; they are intrinsically inferior to women; they are the sole perpetrators of abuse; and they carry all the negative characteristics of the human species.

I chose Critical Theory because the aim of this research was not to obtain an objective account of the interactions between people in conflict, nor to suggest an interpretation of the dynamics. It was to give disempowered men an opportunity to be heard, to be validated, and to gain further insight into their oppression. It was also to analyse how the social structures which work against men have served to increase both their disempowerment and the unwarranted guilt which many of them hold towards women.

The distorted communication which Critical Theory addresses involves ideas which come to be accepted by a society in a manner which precludes critical examination by the individuals affected by them. The workings of the external forces responsible for the generation of these ideas may not be apparent, so the disempowerment is concealed.

Masculinity is a construct with obscure origins. It is predicated on competition and the need to win, a fear of losing face, a fear of being seen to be vulnerable, and a fear of disapproval by others. These requirements of masculinity are rarely challenged by men, who expend enormous amounts of time and energy trying to prove to themselves and to the world that they are successful and are fulfilling their given role.

Society says to men, 'If you perform, you will get love and respect; if you fail, you will be a nothing' (Farrell 1994 p.15). Every man has to strive to reach a position of power and control, where he will be safe. Rich suggests that we have created a society in which men are so fearful of not measuring up that many would rather succeed at suicide than be perceived as failures (Cose 1995 p.198).

Although men hold dominant positions in society, there are only a few who win over others and stay at the top. The remainder are on the periphery. They are lonely, isolated and confused. Men are divided against each other and live in constant fear of humiliation and in fear of other men (Goff 1998 p.5). McLean sees men as competitors rather than allies. 'A "real man" stands alone — alone from women and from other men' (1996 p.16).

Whereas tribal men proved their worth by enduring painful initiating ceremonies, men today have to constantly prove themselves in the workplace. Tacey suggests that in whipping men into a frenzy of over-achievement, tyrannical employers can exacerbate men's performance anxieties and their feelings of low self-worth (1997 p.124).

Women's criticism of men has become so culturally acceptable that if a man tries to defend himself, or males generally, he is accused of sexism and of demeaning women (Arndt 1995 p.221). Women have come to regard themselves as victims, whose only means of achieving justice is to struggle for power against their male oppressors. The justification for the abuse of men by women is that in living in a male dominated world, women are forced to act in this way. Any condemnation of their actions comes from a male frame of reference and is, therefore, unreliable. The ideological presumption which underlies this position is that since men have greater financial resources and hold the most powerful positions in society, they cannot be in the position of victim.

Whereas 'power' is normally defined as control over other people, income and status, Farrell sees it as involving control over our own lives. This includes access to internal rewards and resources such as the capacity for emotional release and a positive self-concept (1986 p.9). A problem for women is that since female powerlessness implies male power, they find it difficult to comprehend the idea of male powerlessness.

When a woman engages in persistent, unprovoked physical and verbal attack, humiliates her partner, forces him to be totally accountable to her, threatens his safety and that of his children, undermines his authority, manipulates him into staying in the relationship, and persuades others (including authority figures) that she, not he, is the victim, she is destroying any sense of personal power and autonomy which the man may once have possessed.

Rather than feeling powerful in their public and private lives, Horrocks says, 'Many men are haunted by feelings of emptiness, impotence and rage. They feel abused, unrecognised by modern society' (1994 p.1). A result of male conditioning is that men are ashamed of owning up to feelings of powerlessness. 'Their identity is fragile; their options are limited; their contributions are discounted; and their very essence is reviled… Most would rather die a thousand horrible deaths than admit that they are in pain' (Cose 1995 p.36). This is reinforced by social attitudes where a cry of help is seen as disgraceful if it comes from a man. Many of the participants were overwhelmed with feelings of shame at their inability to solve the problem of the abuse or to extricate themselves from the situation.

Although women have demanded equal opportunities in employment and career (the traditional male domain), they have been unwilling to grant men equal power in the home (the female domain). Women are still the 'gatekeepers' when it comes to the way the children will be raised and in most aspects of family life. As Horrocks states, 'In our culture there is a visible patriarchy — the economic and social dominance of men over women — and an invisible matriarchy — the emotional dominance of women over men' (1994 p.27). He sees men as occupying a 'no-man's- land', guilty about their traditional areas of power on the one hand, but afraid to go into new areas dominated by women.

The male is seen as potentially violent because of his higher testosterone levels. The justice system imposes penalties for physical violence but not for psychological abuse. Many of the participants felt that the constant denigration they experienced was even more damaging to their self esteem than the episodes of physical attack.

Disempowerment has traditionally been seen as the result of an interaction between powerful and oppressed groups. Whyte suggests that the oppression of men does not fall within this definition. There is no well-identified powerful group which oppresses men. Rather it is the whole of society (1998a p.1).

A similar argument is used by Fauldi when she asks, 'Why don't contemporary men rise up in protest against their betrayal? Why don't they challenge the culture as women did?' Her explanation is not the typical feminist argument that men are unwilling to give up the reins of power. (She feels they have lost that anyway.) Rather it is that whereas women were fighting against something identifiable, male domination, men have no clearly defined enemy. Men cannot be oppressed when the culture has already identified them as the oppressors and when they see themselves that way (1990 p.604).

The participants who reported their abuse to authorities were treated with disdain or disbelief. Alternatively they were blamed for causing the abuse, or encouraged to seek help — of the kind offered to individuals with psychological dysfunction. This 'socially formed pattern arising from human struggle' has resulted in a refusal to accept that the group whose behaviour was allegedly the original cause of the struggle, could now find itself in a situation of oppression.

The process of reflecting on their situation has an emancipatory potential for men. Such an activity, according to Habermas, is fundamental to the way a society functions.

The manner in which I conducted the interviews was felt by participants to be validating and affirming. In expressing my horror at what they had been subjected to, I was giving them the space they needed, both to tell me their story and to express the deep emotions associated with abuse and betrayal. Many of them had few opportunities to speak to anyone in an atmosphere of trust and acceptance.

I was able to share with participants the findings of research which suggests that women are at least as violent as men in the context of their relationships, and also the stories of other men who had been through similar ordeals. In discussing social attitudes I suggested that if I had been in a different profession I would probably never have recognised the pain men are suffering, and would simply have accepted the feminist agenda and the discourse of the superiority of women.

For any group to experience disempowerment, it must be deemed inferior and dangerous. Men are now suffering under the weight of this judgment. Society attributes negative characteristics to males and positive characteristics to females. The former are associated with the worst aspects of a technological society, whereas the latter are seen as its salvation.

In recent years western culture has been strongly influenced by radical feminist theory, which holds that the sexes are adversarially poised. All forms of oppression derive from the power men have over women, which becomes a model for men's pursuit of power over other men as well.

Men are seen as a class of abusers, from which arise individuals with greater or lesser abusive capacity.

This belief is reflected in the American education system, where a doctrine that masculinity is evil and boys should be raised as girls has resulted in boys as young as six being accused of misogyny (Summers 2000, p.8). Daly regards phallocracy as 'the most basic, radical and universal societal manifestation of evil' (1984 p.164). She sees it as the underlying cause of genocide, racism, nuclear and chemical contamination, and spiritual pollution. Men are alleged to behave in a self-satisfied and unrestrained way, and the benefit they receive from patriarchy causes them to perpetuate the system. Daly believes women must regard men as the 'enemy' since they are the planners and controllers of patriarchy, and that women must blame men for the present situation rather than seeing it as the workings of impersonal forces.

A widely-held feminist view is that early matriarchal societies were a form of paradise. Sheaffer refers to a 'feminist fable' based on this idea, in which men alone are responsible for evil and women represent everything good (1997 p.2). Since victimhood is associated with innocence, the alleged moral disparity between the sexes is given even greater credence because of women's past oppression. Taking the moral high ground allows women to act towards men in the roles of judge and executioner. Despite the pain and humiliation experienced by the participants in this study, most of them still held to the idea that 'women are better than men'.

The attitude of some feminists towards men is described by Tacey: 'The penis is linked with rape, manhood is synonymous with violence, maleness is a violation of an innately feminine nature, and indeed masculinity itself is no more than an abominable fiction or construct that "progressive" politics must attempt to destroy' (1997 p.6). He also writes that in most profeminist discourses, the phallus is an organ of shame and guilt and is a symbol of woman's oppression and defilement. Male character and personality is attacked 'as if every man were a terrible rapist or mankind a one-eyed Cyclops' (op.cit. p.50).

Connell discusses a powerful current in feminism which sees masculinity as 'more or less unrelieved villainy'. He feels this leads men into 'a paralyzing politics of guilt' (cited in Tacey 1997 p.50). Sometimes it seems that everything a man does is bad. 'He's the abuser. He's the control freak' (Cose 1995 p.37).

Being seen as the 'bad ones' means that men have difficulty in recovering from their hurts. Thomas suggests that men succumb to feelings of self-hatred when faced with accusations that they are 'bad people who must be blamed for what is wrong with the world and who cannot expect to be treated with kindness or consideration' (1993 p.11).

In Whyte's theory, a result of external, institutionalised oppression is the creation of 'distress recordings'. Past invalidations of a man have the effect on him as if they were still being received and currently invalidating him. Men 'internalise the endless criticism that drenches society' and they feel responsible for everything that is wrong in the world (1998a p.3). This 'internalized oppression' operates so as to have the man believing the negative male stereotypes. It leaves him feeling discouraged, isolated, guilty, depressed, angry, and vulnerable to interacting with other men's negative recordings (1998b p.2). At various times during the period of abuse, most of the participants suffered from depression, despair and emotional withdrawal.

The idea that society's problems are caused by males is reflected in programs for families involved in domestic violence. In the United States the Duluth Model defines battering as 'a conscious strategy by men to assert male dominance over women' (Hoff 1998 p.1). The cause of battery is said to be the fact that men are the beneficiaries of male privilege and they sit on top of a patriarchal power pyramid. Men are 're-educated' about their privileged position until they admit they are responsible for all violence in their relationships. In Washington, a treatment program for both male and female batterers includes an indoctrination course which states that the cause of all violence is men's oppression of women. There is thus a 'blame and shame' approach for male batterers and a 'blame the victim' approach for female batterers.

When men are judged within the context of their intimate relationships and by society as a whole, they experience a violation of their identity.

In a recent development in Critical Theory, Honneth proposes that human identity develops in the social forms of communication in the individual's life experience. An important factor in successful identity formation is emotional concern in an intimate relationship. Intuitive notions of justice are connected with respect for one's own dignity, honour and integrity. The normative presupposition of all communication is to be found in the acquisition of 'social recognition'.

Subjects encounter each other within the parameters of the reciprocal expectation that they will receive recognition as moral persons. When this does not happen, people experience the constriction of their moral point of view, which is experienced as a violation of their identity. Typical responses to such violations are shame, anger and indignation (in Dews (ed.) 1999 p.329).

Whereas some of the participants experienced feelings of worthlessness as a result of their abuse, others expressed outrage at their partner's attempts to hurt and humiliate them. Honneth describes these experiences as feelings of 'social disrespect' (ibid.).

In the formation of male identity, a man is placed in the situation of having to disown his fundamental identity as a human being. To develop a 'self', a person has to experience relationships of intimacy, trust and commitment. The absence of the kind of inner self-validation which arises from such relationships results in an intense need for external approval (Griffith in Boud and Griffin (eds.) 1987 p.52). For a man to pass society's test of 'manhood', he has to be on guard against the judgment of other men, and is thus forced to close down his basic human capacity for empathy (Stoltenberg in Schacht and Ewing (eds.) 1998 p.152). The absence of experiences of empathy works against the development of a strong sense of self.

Whyte suggests that the relationships men form once their emotions are suppressed are based on seeing themselves not as who they are but as what they do. In being conditioned to identify with their work, men do not see their internal reality as of any significance (1998a p.3). Most of the participants said they worked extremely long hours and felt that by doing so they were fulfilling the role expected of them.

As a result of their conditioning, men in society are seen as the 'rational' ones. They are valued for their logic and their ability to accomplish tasks. They will, therefore, tend to focus their efforts on activity which will enhance their masculine identity. Some men in the study reported that although at times they were encouraged by their partners to express their feelings, when they did so, those feelings were often ridiculed. This worked against the development of an identity which would have facilitated the expression of their basic needs.

Despite their attempts to construct a masculine identity, men often feel they have not attained it. Formaini writes, 'Of all the men I see in therapy, not one of them feels himself to be masculine. They feel as though they are failures because they don't measure up to what they believe masculine men ought to be' (1990 p.8). Whyte suggests that the worse a man feels about himself as a man, the more he tends to act from his male role conditioning in order to feel better, but that in acting against his basic nature he increases his sense of self rejection (1997a p.1).

Several participants resented the fact that men are portrayed as aggressive and abusive when they saw themselves as gentle and caring. They felt that since there is only a negative identity given to men by society, it was difficult for them to find a recognisable masculine identity consistent with the qualities they believed they possessed.

When a man is given recognition only in terms of his constructed masculine image, he experiences a form of non-recognition which in Honneth's view constitutes the threat of a loss of personality. Boys are taught about the demands the culture will make on them as men. Formaini believes that defining the male in this way creates a division between the natural process of development and the contrived process which is the outcome of that conditioning.

'Men's emotions and their bodies are separated by a gulf as deep as the split in their internal reality. Because they are trained to be harsh, they are divided from the natural human connection of love and tenderness' (1990 p.37).

The problem of splitting is addressed by McLean, who feels that men are required to maintain discrete islands of consciousness that are mutually incompatible, but that they are completely unaware of the contradictions involved (1996 p.20). Society says that men are supposed to be strong, powerful and courageous, but then they are told that these characteristics are not desirable. Whyte suggests that male sexuality is deemed to be compulsive, impersonal, objectifying, coercive, active, driven to orgasm, proving of manhood. A man has either not enough of this conditioning and he is seen as a 'poof' or he has too much and he's a rapist and a monster. If a man does not fit the stereotype he is considered to possess some personal flaw. The result of these attitudes is that men are confused about their sexual identity.

The social recognition which Honneth describes can be conveyed verbally or through acts of physical contact. Foucault states that bodies became the objects of new disciplinary sciences as new technologies of power brought them under control (Connell 1995 p.49). Men are allowed demonstrations of affection only on the sporting field and within their own families. They are required to exercise extraordinary restraint in the area of dress and general behaviour, so that they are denied the opportunity for a full expression of their humanity. Since the body is an expression of the innermost being, men are forced to exist in a social environment where their basic identity is surrounded with suspicion.

There are no social policies regarding men who are abused by their female partners and consequently there is no help given to them. When official sources suggest that the 'abused man' is a myth, the man himself may wonder whether or not he exists. Several of the participants said that as a result of being invalidated both by their partner and by society, they had contemplated or even attempted suicide.

The man's need for 'emotional concern in an intimate relationship' was cruelly denied by those women who physically attacked their partners. Apart from the injuries received, the man was both fearful for his safety and placed in a situation where he could not find support or help — or even anyone who would believe his story. Some of the women seemed to have a need to make the man into a different person from what he was by constantly taunting him in the hope that he would lose control and violate his own standards of behaviour. This would then force him to call into question his own sense of identity.

A form of treatment which is psychologically destabilising is to place a person in a situation where he is punished for whatever choice he makes. Some of the participants tried to create harmony in their relationships by acceding to all their partner's demands. This failed, however, when the woman found a reason to condemn a particular behaviour on one occasion, only to condemn its opposite on another. The woman in such cases was denying the man's expectations of reciprocal recognition based on an assumption of consistent behaviour. The man experienced confusion and a sense of alienation.

In Honneth's theory, forms of communication are determinants of identity. Common behaviours of abusive women included the complete withdrawal of communication, this form of punishment in some cases lasting for several weeks. Refusal to acknowledge the existence of another person represents a negation of that person's being. The men who were subjected to that treatment experienced it as total rejection.

Despite their programming by society, most men long for a relationship of intimacy and trust. This longing was so intense with some of the participants that they were willing to risk disclosing weaknesses and vulnerabilities to their partner in the hope that this would lead to a strengthening of the relationship. When the woman subsequently used this information to humiliate them, they were overwhelmed by feelings of betrayal.

Those participants who were forced to have sex under threat of punishment or humiliation experienced a violation of their identity at a very deep level. Their view of their own masculinity was seriously challenged, as was their perception of themselves as worthwhile human beings.

They were deprived of any sense of autonomy, self-respect, or the opportunity to enter into an experience of self-giving and mutual enrichment.

The abusive woman's need to exercise total power over the man was evident in situations where he managed to find the kind of help which was affirming of his identity. This was perceived by his partner as a threat to her position of domination and she would increase the level of abuse. The man would then experience an even greater sense of inadequacy in being unable to formulate strategies to resolve the situation.

The development of self esteem is an essential part of the formation of an adequate self concept. In an intimate relationship the partner's opinion is of critical importance in this process. Some women sought to undermine the man's belief in himself through derogatory comments about his appearance, his personality characteristics and his place in the world.

The absence of a secure sense of identity is associated with a problem in defining personal boundaries. An abused man may be unsure as to where his reality ends and his partner's begins. This may cause him to accept his partner's negative view of him, even when there is no evidence to support such a position. The majority of the participants, at the height of the abuse, had come to accept that they were totally responsible for their partner's behaviour, either because of their own inadequacies, or because they had done something to provoke the abuse. The woman had undermined the man's sense of himself to such an extent that he came to see himself through her eyes as 'less than a man', or he no longer had any sense of what it was to be a man.

In applying the principles of Critical Theory, I was seeking to help men understand that they are not inferior to women, they are not responsible for the problems of our civilization, and there is no moral or social justification for their abuse by women.

In contrast to the belief that patriarchy arose from a male obsession with power, Fisher (1979), believes that when the culture changed from hunting and gathering to farming and the domestication of animals, social pressures and material necessity resulted in the need for reproductive control which ended up in the hands of men. Morgan (1982), suggests that women were for the most part responsible for the division of labour which resulted in the present system (cited in Hunter (1993) p.32).

Patriarchy arose also as a result of the evolution in ideas. With the Enlightenment's elevation of reason, the emotions became devalued, and with the scientific discoveries of the 17th century, progress became identified with the domination of nature. Since women were regarded as being closer to nature and also more emotional than rational, men were seen as the natural leaders

(Seidler 1995 pp.27-30). This historical development did not represent some form of conspiracy on the part of men to oppress women. Rather, men drew incorrect conclusions about the relationship between reason and emotions, spirit and matter.

The image of men as violent and dangerous (in comparison with women) is challenged by Thomas (1993), who points out that the group most at risk for homicide in the United Kingdom is that of children under the age of one. Their murderers are mainly women. In New South Wales, between 1968 and 1986, women committed 53.2 per cent of homicides involving victims under ten years of age (Arndt 1995 p.222). Society makes all kinds of allowances for female homicidal acts, but no such compassion is shown towards males. Organisations established to help victims of domestic violence are often staffed by women described by Young as 'gender feminists', who link male violence with patriarchy, but are silent about the high incidence of violence in lesbian relationships (1997 p.2).

A female counsellor writes:

'I've spoken with thousands ... of men who are victims of domestic violence. Knifed, hit over the head with heavy ashtrays, with telephones, pushed through dining room windows, run over, burned, noses broken, beaten, kicked... Men are not the violent time bombs that propaganda lead us to expect; this false image is the result of politicised hysteria and tendentious surveys'
(LFAA 1998 p.8).

McLean describes the dilemmas men face when described as oppressors:

> *'If my sense of identity is deeply tied up with being a man, and men are oppressors, where does that leave me? In seeking change, am I in effect writing myself out of existence? What does it mean to say that men are in a position of power, when I personally feel powerless? And how do I understand the pain, suffering and sense of injustice that I also experience?' (1996 p.13).*

An early feminist theory proposed by de Beauvoir (1953), suggests that the cause of women's subordination is that men are defined as the 'Self', with women placed in the category of the 'Other'. Whether or not that perspective was true for that era, the opposite is now the case with regard to the perceived worth of the sexes. Tacey believes that when one gender [the feminine] becomes 'god-like', the other, by way of archetypal compensation, assumes a demonic appearance (1997 p.24). Since feminists see women being on a higher plane than men, it is the latter who are now designated as 'other'.

Concepts come to be accepted in a society through the emergence of what Foucault describes as 'discourses'. These are shared meanings or bodies of knowledge — 'systematic conceptual frameworks which define their own truth criteria' (Crotty 1998 p.200). They operate largely at the level of the unconscious. Sheaffer believes that the ideas of the 'politically correct feminist movement' have become so much a part of our way of thinking that any critical scrutiny of the feminists' claims amounts to 'blaming the victim', and that in this context a large portion of the educated public has unquestioningly accepted 'a great deal of selective truth, half-truth, and even untruth.' (1997 p.1).

An indication of which discourses have come to form part of our social fabric is the policy and practices of the media. Material will not be presented which could be construed as being negative to women. Men are consistently portrayed as defective or incompetent. They are seen as a threat to women and children, or even worse, as having no real value in their children's lives. Arndt suggests that extremist feminist views on men are regularly promoted, women's groups are given the opportunity to criticise any material which runs counter to feminist arguments, but there is no attempt to allow men to critique feminists' claims (1995 p.225).

The radical feminist position has been criticised on the basis of its essentialism, in that it sees all men as aggressors and all women as victims. The idea that in a democratic society men are the only ones empowered to act, means that women must be either naturally submissive to men, brainwashed by men, or afraid of men. This suggests that women have weaker wills or more fragile psyches — which is at odds with feminist beliefs (Cose 1995 p.13). Curthoys feels that radical feminists' biological determinism leads to a rejection of the ideal of men and women sharing child-rearing on the grounds that since men are evil, children should be reared only by women (1988 p.65).

By deeming men as the 'bad' ones, women have felt free to construct the world of relationships to suit their own purposes. Surveys show that a man's earning potential is the major factor in a woman's attraction to him. Knowing this, men believe their role is to be a good provider. But after fulfilling that role to the best of their ability, many men are rejected because they are not displaying more 'feminine' characteristics. 'They are sneered at for showing their love by doing' (Arndt 1995 p.227).

In today's society many men are powerless, while women are gaining increasing political and financial power. These facts alone expose the fallacy of a power division along gender lines. Also such an approach denies both men and women their individuality and ignores the variety of roles we play in an increasingly complex world. Horrocks points out that feminism is concerned with power relations in the external or the 'real' world. He sees this as a materialist stance in its presupposition that there is an objective material world independent of human consciousness (1994 p.39).

Radical feminism has been linked with Marxism as being a mono-theory since it posits one factor, sex stratification, as the source of all oppression and fails to recognise the socially constructed nature of our attitudes and behaviour. Yeatman challenges the idea of gender identity being assigned a given and prior status. She writes, 'We cannot know who we are until we act and our action always takes place in a particular context of relationship' (in Caine and Pringle (eds.) 1995 p.55).

Some sociologists have criticised the theory as representing 'another form of the naturalistic fallacy of Rousseau in that it sees woman as nature and man as culture, labels all social problems "culture" and then advocates overthrowing culture for the liberation of women' (Hunter 1993 p.3). 'Patriarchy oppresses… to the detriment of all life on this planet' (Hunter 1993 p.19). This statement suggests that patriarchy is not a system in which one group (men) enjoy all the benefits of civilization through their exercise of power over another group (women). Rather, patriarchy is a system which evolved as a result of changing material circumstances and developments in the history of thought. Historically it has brought great benefits and great losses. The benefits have been external — higher standards of living, increased life expectancy.

The losses have been internal — the devaluing of the emotions, the reduction of the spiritual to the material, and the destruction of our deepseated connections to the planet. These losses are unrelated to gender.

Tacey describes certain feminists seeking the overthrow of patriarchy as 'motivated by revenge and the desire to find a scapegoat for human evil' (1997 p.41). He believes that those who see only men's power and not men's suffering become intolerant, moralistic, punishing and guilt-ridden. Feminists' statements that the phallus is a symbol of woman's oppression and defilement, Tacey regards as indicative of psychic disturbance (op.cit. p.51). In analysing the effects of 'politically correct feminism', Sheaffer refers to Nietzsche's warning against systems of morality grounded in what he called ressentiment, which embody the covert destructiveness of those who desire revenge against those they envy (1997 p.8)

Daly's theory that men have an innate need to act in an unrestrained and self-satisfied way in exerting power over women, cannot be sustained in the light of the fact that boys are under severe social pressure in the process of their conditioning as males. This conditioning involves a ruthless suppression of their feminine side and the adoption of behaviours which are basically alien to them. Even theorists who are sympathetic to the plight of men today find it difficult to rid themselves of the idea that 'men have all the power'. They are assuming that since there are more males than females in positions of authority, males will make decisions and create policies favourable to men. Even if the foregoing were true in respect of the corporate world and large institutions, it does not hold in the area of public policy. It is not reflected in the treatment of men by government departments and instrumentalities and by the legal system. Males in positions of power in the public sphere have so absorbed the feminist agenda that they are in fact being patriarchal in the sense of being dominant and intolerant, but it is a 'feminist patriarchy' which is being imposed.

Because of the shift in the perception of men and the prejudice against them in the public domain, women are now in a position of being able to exploit that power to the detriment of men. A woman can abuse a man with impunity, since she knows he will have little, if any, recourse in the legal system, and that in the event of a breakdown in the relationship, she will have custody of the children and can use them as a weapon against her partner.

The above will be seen as a disparaging view of women, but it compares favourably with the radical feminists' view of men. The reality is that the majority of men and women seek to develop loving relationships with their partners and their children. Where a relationship runs into difficulty and one partner engages in abusive behaviour, the causes will most likely include unresolved problems in the abusive person's family of origin. Although I have not found any research which confirms this hypothesis, the anecdotal evidence from case histories strongly supports it.

There are certain aspects of human personality which have come to be regarded as feminine. Since these qualities are the ones which the patriarchal system requires men to suppress, patriarchy can be seen as more psychologically damaging to men than it is to women. Horrocks writes that the men who see him in therapy say to him, 'to become the man I was supposed to be, I had to destroy my most vulnerable side, my sensitivity, my femininity, my creativity' (1994 p.25).

In Jungian thought, the 'shadow' consists of those characteristics which people fear and despise and cannot accept within themselves. Where the shadow is not acknowledged by the individual, its contents are projected on to others, who are then deemed to possess those undesirable traits. Although the shadow is basically personal, groups of people and whole societies can have a collective shadow, through which other groups are designated as inferior. Groups which have been the recipients of this kind of projection include Jews, gypsies, blacks and homosexuals.

Radical feminists and others in society are projecting a collective shadow on to men, based on a simplistic form of reasoning: men are psychologically and spiritually inadequate; they have all the power; therefore, their failures are the cause of all the problems in civilization. As is the case with all group projections, whether they have a racial, class or gender basis, the more the proponents of patriarchal feminism project their shadow, the less they recognise their own impoverishment, and the more the objects of their projection sink under its weight.

In such a situation men can project their shadow on to other men. Instead of distinguishing between good and bad forms of masculinity, they can come to accept that masculinity itself is evil. One of the reasons for abused men finding no help in society, and instead being accused of abusive behaviour themselves, is that male judges, barristers, psychiatrists, police officers and public officials will go to extraordinary lengths to assist women who make false allegations of abuse by men, even to the point of fabricating evidence on their behalf. Many of the participants suffered from this form of injustice.

In an archetypal analysis of what is happening in society today, Tacey states that we have moved from a Zeus-like liberational pattern, where the father is tricked into releasing all the forms and figures he has devoured, to a new mythic territory where the emphasis is upon killing the father. The former is a creative act;

the latter leads to Oedipal regression and incestuous coupling with the maternal source. When society is caught in the Oedipal mode, it does not move beyond the father after killing him, but moves back into a chaotic, pre-patriarchal age where the father's order is absent and consciousness is ruined (1997 pp.49-50).

The idealisation of the maternal and the feminine involves the lack of recognition of the 'devouring' nature of the maternal archetype. Tacey believes men need to develop enough masculine potential to stand against the might of the primal feminine, symbolised by the dragon mother.

When male or female public officials disempower men, they are murdering the archetypal father. When sections of the men's movement allow themselves to experience a collective guilt because they happen to have been born male, and at the same time seek to suppress their masculine characteristics, they are succumbing to the power of the archetypal feminine. This can also happen when men allow women to abuse them on the basis that there is something inherently lacking in masculinity.

Critical social theorists believe that ideology can become a form of false consciousnes in that it supports unjust social practices (Mezirow 1990 p.15). Ideology can cause the members of the oppressed category to believe that there is something intrinsic and natural about the way they are treated, rather than something socially constructed (Hunter 1993 p.5). People in an 'enlightened' society believe that equality before the law is fundamental to its political and social philosophy. Such equality, they would claim, extends to an individual's dealings with government and public institutions. Where there is a discrepancy between official policy and the manner in which it is implemented, it can be even more difficult for disempowered individuals to realise that they are, in fact, part of an oppressed group, and that the unacknowledged policies and practices which work against them have arisen because of a perception in society that they deserve exactly what they get. Just as in the more traditional cases of oppression, men can also come to believe that there is something 'intrinsic and natural' about the way they are treated.

Critical Theory's task is to assist in raising the consciousness of disempowered people so that they no longer conspire in their own oppression. People can be unaware of their oppression because of the effects of their socialisation. In the lives of males, this socialisation begins at a young age, when the boy leaves the security of the maternal world to forge an uncertain identity which is forever under challenge, the essence of that identity being regarded with perpetual suspicion.

One of the difficulties in helping men to understand their oppression is connected with another aspect of that conditioning. Males are taught that to be a man means to be a winner — in every area of life. Several participants said to me, 'I will tell you my story, but only on the condition that you do not describe me as a victim. I don't see myself that way. I made a bad choice and I lived with the consequences'. In those cases it was not possible for me to do any 'consciousness raising'. The man would have experienced it as a challenge to his masculinity.

Many of the participants felt that there was something fundamentally wrong with our social structure, but they believed that the forces against them would make any protest futile. The lack of response to their abuse had made them distrustful of authority. Originally they believed that there was some basic moral law on which our society is built. Having lost faith in the system, some of them also said they had ceased to believe in the concept of morality.

The principles they once taught their children they felt they could no longer live by.

In their experiences of disempowerment, judgment and identity violation, the men expressed various emotions, but the most poignant and distressing to me as a researcher was their sense of hopelessness and betrayal. In telling these men that I would publish their stories, I felt I was giving them some faint hope that the world could become a better place. I suggested to them that there are now many people who believe what they are saying and who will do everything they can to bring that knowledge to the wider community.

Having come to some understanding of the pain men suffer, I was unprepared for the anger I felt, not towards those women who refused to believe the depths to which our sex can sink, but to those men who were not part of the project but who made the comment, 'Men have it made. We don't need a men's movement. Those men you interviewed — they were just losers.'

Conclusion

My hypotheses were confirmed concerning both men's suffering at the hands of their female partners and also the prejudices of society. However, I underestimated both the extent of the suffering and the degree of discrimination against men by the police, the courts and child welfare agencies, and in the overall implementation of public policy.

In giving abused men a voice and the opportunity to tell their stories in an atmosphere of trust, I went on a journey of discovery. As an abused person, I was giving myself a voice. The men's pain became my pain, their injustice my injustice, their anger my anger. I listened to myself as I listened to them, and in helping to free them, I freed myself. My inner processes were facilitated by the validation which I as a woman receive from society, and I sought to bring something of that hope and vision to the men whose stories I was privileged to share.

In support groups all over the country, men are learning about their emotional life. They are seeking the kind of inner freedom which women rightly enjoy. But the fight for their emancipation is not theirs alone. Just as men in positions of power originally gave women their social and political rights, so women today must exercise their power in standing for the rights of those men who are struggling against overwhelming odds, and whose pain has no name.

'Modern man's aspirations include not only liberation from exterior pressures which prevent his fulfilment as a member of a certain social class, country or society. He seeks likewise an interior liberation, in an individual and intimate dimension; he seeks liberation not only on a social plane but also on a psychological. He seeks an interior freedom understood however not as an ideological evasion from social responsibility or as the internalization of a situation of dependency. Rather it must be in relation to the real world of the human psyche'

(Gutierrez 1974 p.30).

Bibliography

Arndt, B. (1995) Taking Sides: Men, Women and the Shifting Social Agenda, Sydney, Random House.

Arndt, B. 'For better or worth', Sydney Morning Herald, 19 August 2000.

Biddulph, S. (1995) Manhood, Sydney, Finch Publishing.

Connell, R. (1995) Masculinities, Sydney, Allen & Unwin.

Cook, P. (1997) Abused Men: The Hidden Side of Domestic Violence, Westport, Praeger.

Cose, E. (1995) A Man's World: How Real is Male Privilege and How High is Its Price?, New York, Harper Collins.

Crotty, M. (1998) The Foundations of Cultural Research, Sydney, Allen & Unwin.

Curthoys, A. (1988) For and Against Feminism, Sydney, Allen & Unwin.

Daly, M. (1984) Pure Lust, London, The Women's Press.

Daly, M. and M. Wilson, 'Parent-offspring homicides in Canada, 1974-1983' in Science (1988, 242).

De Beauvoir, S. (1953) The Second Sex, London, Pan.

Dews, P. (ed.) (1999) Habermas: A Critical Reader, Oxford, Blackwell.

Easton, S. (1998) Three Steps to Avoid Being a Victim of Domestic Violence, Eastern Alliance Educational Series Vol. 1.6.

Eldridge, R. (1998) 'The Male Victim' in Battered Men: The Hidden Side of Domestic Violence

Farmer, S. (1991) The Wounded Male, New York, Ballantine.

Farrell, W. (1986) Why Men are the Way They Are, New York, McGraw Hill.

Farrell, W. (1994) The Myth of Male Power, Sydney, Random House.

Fauldi, S. (1999) Stiffed: The Betrayal of the Modern Man, London, Chatto and Windus.

Fiebert, M. (1998) Spousal Violence Scientific Research Citations. An Annotated Bibliography.

Fine, M. 'Working the Hyphens: Reinventing Self and Other in Qualitative Research, in Handbook of Qualitative Research', N. Denzin and Y. Lincoln (eds) (1994), London, Sage.

Fisher, E. (1979) Women's Creation: Sexual Evolution and the Shaping of Society, New York, McGraw Hill.

Formaini, H. (1990) Men: The Darker Continent, London, Heinemann.

Goff, T. 'Behind Closed Doors: A focus on men' in Relationships Australia (NSW) Conference on Domestic Violence, 1998.

Green, M. (1998) Fathers After Divorce, Sydney, Finch Publishing.

Gregorash, L. (1993) Family Violence: An Exploratory Study of Men Who Have Been Abused by Their Wives, master's thesis, University of Calgary.

Griffith, G. 'Images of Interdependence: Authority and Power in Teaching/Learning' in D. Boud and V. Griffin (eds.) (1987) Appreciating Adults' Learning: From the Learners' Perspective, London, Kogan Page.

Gross, D. (1992) Class Notes on Husband Battering.

Guiterriez, G. (1974) A Theology of Liberation, London, SCM.

Hoff, B. and R. Easterbrooks (1998) 'The Ultra-Sensitive Man' in Battered Men — The Hidden Side of Domestic Violence.

Hoff, B. (1998) 'The Duluth Model' in Battered Men — The Hidden Side of Domestic Violence.

Hoff, B. (1999) 'What is Abuse?' in Battered Men: The Hidden Side of Domestic Violence.

Honneth, A. 'The social dynamics of disrespect: situating Critical Theory today' in P. Dews (ed.)(1999) Habermas: A Critical Reader, Oxford, Blackwell.

Horrocks, R. (1994) Masculinity in Crisis, London, Macmillan.

Hunter, A. (1993) The Radical Feminist Perspective in the Field of Sociology.

Krieger, S. (1991) Social Science and the Self, New Brunswick, Rutgers.

Le Compte, M. 'Emergent Paradigms: How New? How Necessary?' in E. Guba (ed.) (1990), The Paradigm Dialog, California, Sage.

Lone Fathers' Association (Australia) Inc. (1998) Comments on Model Domestic Violence Legislation.

McLean, C., 'The Politics of Men's Pain' in C. McLean, M. Carey and C. White (1996) Men's Ways of Being, London, Westview Press.

McNeely, R. and G. Robinson-Simpson (1988) 'The truth about domestic violence: A falsely framed issue' in Gender Sanity, University Press of America.

Mezirow, J. 'How Critical Reflection Triggers Transformative Learning' in J. Mezirow and Associates (1990) Fostering Critical Reflection in Adulthood, San Francisco, Jossey-Bass.

Mignon, S., 'Husband Battering: A Review of the Debate over a Controversial Social Phenomenon' in Violence in Intimate Relationships (1998) Boston, Butterworth-Heinemann.

Murray, A. and A. Blackmore (1993) 'Influences on Parent-child Relationships in Non-custodial Fathers' in Australian Journal of Marriage & Family, Vol. 14, No. 3, p.154.

O'Connor, P. (1993) The Inner Man, Sydney, Pan Macmillan.

O'Donnel, K. (1994) Battered men: insiders view.

Olesen, V. 'Feminisms and models of qualitative research' in N. Denzin & Y. Lincoln (eds.)(1994) Handbook of Qualitative Research, London, Sage.

Peloche, M. (1999) 'Does Husband Abuse Exist?', unpublished essay submitted to Charles Sturt University.

Rowan, J. 'The psychology of science by Abraham Maslow: an appreciation' in P. Reason and J. Rowan (eds.)(1981) Human Inquiry Bath, Wiley.

Sarantakos, S. (1998) 'Husband abuse as self-defence', paper presented at the International Congress of Sociology, Montreal, Canada.

Sarantakos, S. 'Husband abuse: Fact or fiction?' in Australian Journal of Social Issues, August 1999.

Seidler, V. (1994) Recovering the Self, New York, Routledge.

Sheaffer, R. (1995, revised in 1997) 'Feminism, the Noble Lie' in Free Inquiry, Vol. 15, No. 2.

Smith, J. 'Alternative Research Paradigms and the Problem of Criteria' in E. Guba (ed.) (1990), The Paradigm Dialog, California, Sage.

Smith, S. (1998) Involuntary Child Absence Syndrome and Depression in Males After Relationship Breakdown, unpublished B.A. (Hons.) thesis, Central Queensland University.

Sniechowski, J. and J. Sherven (1995) Blaming Men Doesn't Stop Domestic Violence.

Stoltenberg, J. 'Healing from Manhood' in S. Schacht and D. Ewing (eds.) (1998) Feminism and Men: Reconstructing Gender Relations, New York University Press.

Summers, C. 'The Gender Project: The Social Experiment That's Destroying Masculinity' in Sunday Magazine (Sunday Telegraph) 9 July 2000.

Tacey, D. (1997) Remaking Men: The Revolution in Masculinity, Melbourne, Penguin.

Thomas, D. (1993) Not Guilty/In Defence of the Modern Man, London, Weidenfeld and Nicolson.

Whyte, P. (1997a) Conditioning, Men and a Changing Culture.

Whyte, P. (1998a) An Introduction to Men's Liberation, http://www.peerleadership.com.au/

Woodstra, K., Under Attack: The lonely cry of battered husbands, 'The Toronto Sun', 7 September 1994.

Young, C. (1997) No excuse for domestic violence.

About the Author

Lynne Renoir suffered physical abuse at the hands of her judgmental father. The pain she endured led her to investigate how other abused people suffer, particularly men in their relationships with destructive women.

In her Master's thesis Lynne interviewed forty-eight men from Australia and New Zealand. They told her about severe physical, psychological and sexual abuse. This led her to the view that men, as a whole, have been disempowered. She points to the fact that society sees only women as victims of abuse, with men inevitably portrayed as perpetrators. Her call is for governmental authorities to recognize the plight of men in abusive relationships and to take action to remedy the wrong that has been done to them.

Lynne can be contacted through her website
www.lynnerenoir.com

God Interrogated –
Reinterpreting the Divine

In this work, Lynne Renoir questions the traditional view of God as an all-powerful being who created the universe and governs it according to his will. She argues that such an idea can be challenged philosophically, and that it does not accord with discoveries in modern science. On the other hand, she suggests, it is evident that experiences of transformation can occur in the lives of individuals who wholeheartedly embrace religious beliefs.

God Interrogated explores possible explanations for this situation by proposing that truth is found in the inner dimensions of a person's being, and is not something that can be imposed from an external source.

Lynne Renoir's work was the result of her own difficulties in experiencing the transformation she sought through her Christian faith, and followed years of research undertaken in the areas of philosophy, psychology, and quantum science.

God Interrogated - Reinterpreting the Divine
is published by John Hunt and will be available in Spring 2023.
Read Lynne Renoir's blog posts and download excerpts from her books at
www.lynnerenoir.com

Leaving Faith, Finding Meaning
A Preacher's Daughter's Search for God

Lynne Renoir was born into a fundamentalist Christian family where the Bible was the central focus. She was not allowed to make mistakes or to challenge her father's opinions. Such behavior, in his view, was the work of Satan. As God's representative in the family, her father believed it was his duty to belt the devil out of his daughter, and he did so regularly and severely.

When the beatings continued into her twenties, Lynne finally broke free. Convinced she was a failure as a believer, she left home, and for several decades she endeavored to live by the tenets of the faith in which she had been raised.

Then when she was fifty, Lynne had an amazing experience of communication with beings in the spirit world. Under their guidance she completed a Master's degree in Psychology and a PhD in Philosophy. She then investigated quantum theory and mysticism, coming to the conclusion that everything in the universe is one. This led her to question the idea of an external, all-powerful being who sits in judgment on his creatures.

For Lynne, the experience of realizing the oneness of all reality has been life transforming. In sharing her fascinating journey from religious indoctrination to spiritual freedom, she reveals a way to those who are seeking to find their own pathway to liberation.

Leaving Faith, Finding Meaning
Available as a paperback from Amazon.com
and in digital format for all E-readers including Kindle

Read Lynne Renoir's blog posts and download excerpts from her books at
www.lynnerenoir.com

Milton Keynes UK
Ingram Content Group UK Ltd.
UKHW010857030424
440506UK00016B/2201